THE BEST

AIR FRYER RECIPES ON THE PLANET

OVER 125 EASY, FOOLPROOF FRIED FAVORITES WITHOUT ALL THE FAT

ELLA SANDERS

CASTLE POINT BOOKS
NEW YORK

THE BEST AIR FRYER RECIPES ON THE PLANET
Copyright © 2018 by St. Martin's Press.

All rights reserved.

Printed in the United States of America. For information,
address St. Martin's Press, 175 Fifth Avenue, New York, N.Y. 10010.

www.castlepointbooks.com

www.stmartins.com

The Castle Point Books trademark is owned by Castle Point Publications, LLC.
Castle Point books are published and distributed by St. Martin's Press.

ISBN 978-1-250-18729-1 (paperback)
ISBN ISBN 978-1-250-18728-4 (ebook)

Photography by Allan Penn.
Special thanks to Jennifer Calvert.

Our books may be purchased in bulk for promotional, educational, or business use.
Please contact your local bookseller or the Macmillan Corporate and Premium Sales Department
at 1-800-221-7945, extension 5442, or by e-mail at MacmillanSpecialMarkets@macmillan.com.

First Edition: May 2018
10 9 8 7 6 5 4 3 2 1

CONTENTS

INTRODUCTION

Life doesn't seem to slow down, so you don't have time to make the healthy food you know you should be eating. When you're on your way home after a long day, the drive thru starts calling your name. But what if you didn't have to choose between what's good *for* you and what tastes good *to* you? And what if you could make it in no time at all?

Thanks to technology, finding ways to stay healthy is only becoming easier in this era of time crunches and multitasking. The air fryer—a small, sit-anywhere appliance—is set to revolutionize the way we make our meals.

Air fryers work by evenly circulating hot air to cook fresh or frozen foods, which gives them the same crunchy bite and tender interiors produced by conventional deep fryers without the need to submerge your food in cooking oils. In other words, the air is the oil, and the frying oil isn't necessary!

The air fryer is a completely closed, all-in-one, nonstick system, which means it's safe for beginners and easy to clean. Just think—no more pots of hot oil sitting dangerously on the stove, splattering all over the place.

And don't be fooled by the name—the air fryer can also roast, steam, grill, and bake. In addition to all of your favorite fried foods, you can make dishes such as mouthwatering Marinated Skirt Steak (page 71), heavenly Honey-Glazed Carrots (page 89), and decadent Double Chocolate Macadamia Nut Brownies (page 136). The bonus being it does all this without the added fat and time-consuming cleanup of ordinary methods. It'll become your go-to cooking appliance in no time!

In this book, you'll find more than 120 recipes to get you started on your journey to quicker, healthier cooking. These include guilt-free appetizers, satisfying snacks, complete meals, and indulgent desserts.

Don't be afraid to tweak the recipes to your needs, or even create new ones. The Quick-Reference Cooking Chart on pages 148–149 will help with this; it provides air frying temperatures and cooking times for several common foods.

So go have some fun with your amazing new appliance, and enjoy your newfound free time!

HOW TO USE YOUR AIR FRYER

Inside the air fryer unit is a removable heating chamber and a cooking basket. To take the cooking basket out of the heating chamber, just press the release button and lift it out.

Many air fryers also come with a removable rack, used for keeping meats off the bottom of the basket, or for steaming items with a little liquid underneath. Some air fryers even come with a baking pan for pizzas and desserts. If you don't have a baking pan especially for your air fryer, you can use a glass, silicone, or oven-safe metal dish instead. No matter which you use, place it in the basket before cooking.

To cook items in your air fryer, just toss them in the basket and select the time and temperature. Some air fryers even have presets for specific kinds of food. If you don't have a certain preset, you'll find a handy chart on pages 148–149 that covers some common foods and their cook times and temperatures.

Whether or not you'll need to preheat your air fryer depends on which model you have, so check the instructions that came with yours. In general, preheating isn't necessary. But when it is, it only takes about 3 minutes.

SAFETY

Air fryers are powerful machines, so make sure you follow safety recommendations.

- Air fryers get extremely hot—especially if you've added oil or steaming liquid to the pan. While your food cooks, liquids will accumulate in the cooking chamber, so always use caution when removing the basket. After the cooking cycle is complete, the basket will be very hot. So after removing it, make sure you place it only on heatproof surfaces.

- Before cooking anything, make sure all the ingredients are inside the air fryer basket to prevent any contact with the heating element.

- During the cooking cycle, hot air or steam is released through the air outlets. Be sure to keep your hands and face away from them. Don't place anything on top of the appliance during operation, and don't cover the air inlets or outlets.

- Don't use the appliance if there is any damage to the plug, electrical cord, or any other parts. In addition, don't use the air fryer (or plug it in) with wet hands, and don't leave it unattended while it's in operation. Make sure to unplug the fryer when it's not in use.

AIR FRYER CARE

Air fryers are small and can live wherever is most convenient. Just make sure you put your air fryer on a flat, even, and stable surface. Leave at least 5 inches of free space around the back, sides, and top of the appliance to allow for adequate air flow.

Always wait 30 minutes for the air fryer to cool down before handling or cleaning it.

You should clean the air fryer after every use by wiping down the outside with a moist cloth, by cleaning the heating chamber and cooking basket by hand with soap and water in the kitchen sink, and by cleaning the inside of the appliance with a damp (wrung-out), nonabrasive sponge, wiping away any food debris and grease. Never clean any part of an air fryer with metal kitchen utensils or abrasive cleaning materials because they can damage the nonstick coating. If there's debris stuck to the basket or bottom of the pan, simply soak it in hot, soapy water for about 10 minutes to loosen it up before cleaning. If necessary, you can clean the heating element (when it's completely cool!) with a wet brush.

COOKING TIPS

Air fryers are easy to use, but here are some tips for making sure you get the most out of yours.

- Any food that can be cooked in a microwave or oven can be cooked in an air fryer.

- To give food a crispy texture, spray cooking oil or nonstick spray over the ingredients before adding them to the basket. Alternatively, you can add a small amount (3–4 tablespoons) of oil to the pan before cooking. (Never overfill, as this will damage the air fryer.)

- Smaller ingredients usually require a slightly shorter cooking time than larger ingredients. Shaking smaller ingredients halfway during the cooking time ensures they'll be evenly cooked.

- To steam food, add a small amount (3–4 tablespoons) of liquid, such as water or broth, to the pan after adding the ingredients. (Never overfill, as this will damage the air fryer.)

- You can also use an air fryer to reheat food by setting the temperature to 300°F for up to 10 minutes.

- See the Quick-Reference Cooking Chart on pages 148–149 for a cheat sheet on how long to cook most foods.

CHAPTER ONE
APPETIZING STARTERS

FRIED MAC AND CHEESE

SERVES 4–6

If you thought mac and cheese couldn't get any better, just wait until you've made it breaded, fried, and bite-sized. Every bit of this classic comfort food turned appetizer whips up quickly in an air fryer, making it the perfect recipe to break in your cooking unit!

Olive oil cooking spray

1½ cups elbow macaroni, uncooked

1 cup chicken broth

½ cup heavy cream

3/4 cup shredded Cheddar cheese

½ cup freshly shredded mozzarella cheese

¼ cup freshly grated Parmesan cheese

Kosher salt and freshly ground black pepper, to taste

2 large eggs, beaten

1 cup Homestyle Breadcrumbs (see page 146)

Spray a cake pan with cooking spray and add the macaroni, broth, cream, cheeses, and salt and pepper. Mix the ingredients together and place the pan in the center of the basket.

Air fry for 30 minutes at 350°F, or until the mac and cheese is bubbling and golden brown. Set aside to cool.

When cool, scoop out approximately 2 tablespoons of the mac and cheese and roll into a ball shape. Set aside on a cookie sheet. Repeat until you've run out of mac and cheese. Place the pan in the refrigerator until the balls are firm, approximately 4 hours.

Remove the balls from the refrigerator and dip each into the beaten egg, then roll it into the breadcrumbs to coat evenly.

Spray each ball with cooking spray before adding it to the basket. Air fry at 400°F for 10 minutes per batch, or until golden.

MOZZARELLA STICKS

SERVES 4–6

Looking for something quick and easy to tide the kids over until dinner? Or need a great appetizer to serve your guests? You won't find a simpler or more scrumptious recipe than this one. Serve these up with Marinara Dipping Sauce (see page 131).

1 (12-ounce) package mozzarella string cheese

2 cups Italian Breadcrumbs (see page 146)

¼ cup freshly grated Parmesan cheese

¼ cup all-purpose flour

2 large eggs, beaten

Olive oil cooking spray

Remove the cheese from the individually wrapped packages and stack them on a cutting board. With a sharp knife, slice the sticks in half, or thirds, depending on the size you like. Place the sticks on a cookie sheet covered in parchment paper, and put the sheet in the freezer, covered with plastic wrap, for 2 hours.

Mix together the breadcrumbs and Parmesan cheese.

Immediately upon removing the sticks from the freezer, roll them first in the flour, then the beaten eggs, then the breadcrumb-Parmesan mixture. As you prepare them, place them back on the cookie sheet you used to freeze them until they're all ready.

Place the sticks in the air fryer basket, making sure they don't touch. Spray the sticks with cooking spray all around, then place the basket into the air fryer.

Air fry for 3 minutes at 400°F, then remove and carefully flip. Air fry for an additional 3–4 minutes, or until golden.

TRADITIONAL ARANCINI

SERVES 4–6

Arancini may sound fancy, but it's an appetizer your whole family will love—cheesy rice balls fried to a delicious golden-brown crispiness. To finish off the Traditional Arancini, serve them with Marinara Dipping Sauce (see page 131).

RISOTTO

1 tablespoon unsalted butter

½ medium Spanish onion, finely chopped

2 garlic cloves, minced

½ cup dry white wine

1 cup Arborio rice

4 cups low-sodium chicken broth, warmed, plus additional as needed

¼ cup freshly grated Parmesan cheese

Kosher salt, to taste

¼ teaspoon freshly ground black pepper

RICE BALLS

2 cups risotto

½ cup Gruyère cheese, cut into ½-inch cubes

1 cup all-purpose flour

2 large eggs, beaten

1 cup Panko Breadcrumbs (see page 147)

Olive oil cooking spray

TO MAKE THE RISOTTO:

Melt the butter in a large saucepan over medium heat. Then add the onion and garlic, stirring well and cooking about 5–6 minutes, until the ingredients are softened and golden.

Stir in the wine and cook another 4 minutes, until the wine is nearly evaporated. Then add the rice and stir until well coated.

Add a ½ cup of the broth and stir well, scraping the bottom and sides of the pan, and cook until it has been absorbed by the rice. Continue adding the broth, a ½ cup at a time as the liquid is absorbed, stirring well after each addition. If rice is still tough, add additional broth until tender.

Stir in the Parmesan, salt, and pepper and remove from the heat. To accelerate cooling, remove the risotto from the saucepan and place in a bowl.

TO MAKE THE RICE BALLS:

When the risotto has cooled, scoop approximately 2 tablespoons into the palm of your hand. Place a cube of Gruyère in the middle, then roll into a ball, making sure to close the cheese completely into the ball. Repeat with remaining risotto.

Roll each of the balls in the flour, dip into the beaten egg, and then roll into the breadcrumbs, coating evenly.

Spray each ball with cooking spray before adding to the basket. Leave space between the rice balls. Air fry at 400°F for 10 minutes per batch, or until golden.

GREEK-STYLE ARANCINI
SERVES 4–6

Spinach and feta cheese give these cheesy rice balls a distinctly Greek spin. If you're running short on time, use a quick-cooking packaged risotto from the store. But if you want something homemade, whip up the risotto used in the Traditional Arancini recipe on page 5.

1 tablespoon olive oil

1 large shallot, chopped

1 (10-ounce) package frozen chopped spinach, thawed and drained

½ cup crumbled feta cheese

2 cups risotto (or short-grain white rice), cooked and well cooled

1 cup all-purpose flour

2 large eggs, beaten

1 cup Panko Breadcrumbs (see page 147)

Olive oil cooking spray

Heat the olive oil in a medium saucepan. Add the shallots and sauté until golden.

Add the spinach and sauté with the shallots until the flavors mix, about 2–3 minutes. Drain excess liquid. Stir in the feta, and set the mixture aside to cool.

Scoop approximately 2 tablespoons of the risotto onto the palm of your hand and flatten.

Add about a teaspoon of the spinach-feta filling, then carefully pack it into a ball shape. Repeat with the remaining risotto and filling.

Roll each of the balls in the flour, dip them into the beaten egg, and then roll them in the breadcrumbs, coating evenly.

Spray each ball with cooking spray before adding to the basket. Air fry at 400°F for 10 minutes per batch, or until golden.

FRIED RAVIOLI

SERVES 6–8

These tasty pasta poppers are so yummy and simple to make, they'll be your new go-to for any impromptu gathering. And if you keep a package of pre-made ravioli in the freezer, you'll be ready anytime. Serve these up with Marinara Dipping Sauce (see page 131) for an instant hit.

24 cheese ravioli, frozen

2 cups all-purpose flour

3 large eggs, beaten

2 cups Homestyle Breadcrumbs (see page TK)

Olive oil cooking spray

Dredge each frozen piece of ravioli in flour, dip it into the beaten egg, and then into the breadcrumbs, pressing on each side to coat evenly.

Spray the breaded ravioli with olive oil, then place them in the basket, leaving space between them.

Air fry in batches at 380°F until golden brown, about 20 minutes.

TINY TOAST WITH VEGGIE SPREAD

SERVES 4–6

If you're craving the taste of sesame stir-fry, these toast bites are sure to satisfy. The beauty of Tiny Toast with Veggie Spread is you can make it suit your needs—choose your favorite fresh veggies, buy a packaged mix, or even use up leftovers.

1 cup diced vegetables, cooked

2 garlic cloves, minced

1 tablespoon cornstarch

1 teaspoon sesame oil

1/4 teaspoon salt

6 tablespoons sesame seeds

6 slices white bread, cut into quarters on the diagonal

Canola oil cooking spray

Combine the first 5 ingredients in a food processor, and pulse them into a fine paste.

Pour the sesame seeds onto a plate or a clean work surface.

Spread the vegetable mixture onto one side of each of the slices of bread. Press the bread into the seeds, vegetable side down, so the seeds cling to the vegetable mixture. Spray the seeded sides of the triangles with cooking spray.

Air fry the triangles at 390°F until golden brown, about 5-8 minutes.

CHEESY GREEK-STYLE POCKETS

SERVES 2–4

Four cheeses come together with delicate puff pastry for a heavenly take on the traditional Greek Tiropitakia. Serve these up with Fiery Cucumber Sauce (see page 141) for a mouthwatering Mediterranean appetizer.

2 cups crumbled feta cheese

1⅓ cups freshly grated Parmesan cheese

1 cup shredded Gruyère cheese

½ cup ricotta cheese

¾ cup heavy cream

½ teaspoon freshly ground black pepper

8 (14- x 18-inch) sheets of frozen phyllo (filo) dough, thawed

¼ cup extra virgin olive oil, divided

2 large eggs, beaten

In a large bowl, mix together the cheeses, cream, and pepper. Cover and refrigerate for 30 minutes.

Spread out 4 of the phyllo dough sheets on a clean work surface, and brush the tops with oil. Top each of these sheets with an additional sheet, and brush these tops with oil as well. Taking both sheets, fold the dough in half lengthwise so that you have a long sheet with one of the short ends closest to you.

With the tip of your finger or a brush, apply a small amount of the beaten egg to all the edges of one of the dough sheets, like a frame.

Spoon about 2 heaping tablespoons of the cheese mixture onto the dough, at the top right, just under where you brushed the egg. Then fold the top left corner of the dough diagonally over it, creating a triangle with the filling underneath. Press the edges to seal the dough.

Carefully fold this filled triangle straight down, then diagonally down to the left, then straight down, then diagonally down to the right, repeating until you have used the rest of the dough sheet. Repeat steps 3 through 5 with remaining dough sheets.

Brush the outside of the filled triangles with the remaining olive oil. Place them in the basket, leaving space around each one.

Air fry in batches (if necessary) at 360°F until golden brown, about 15 minutes. Let the triangles cool for about 20 minutes before serving to allow the cheese to set.

HERBED RICOTTA BITES

SERVES 4–6

Herbed Ricotta Bites are fried ravioli gone gourmet! Ricotta cheese gets wrapped up in a crispy shell of breadcrumbs and Italian herbs for a burst of flavor in every cheesy bite.

1 cup ricotta cheese

2 tablespoons all-purpose flour

½ teaspoon dried thyme

½ teaspoon dried rosemary, crushed

½ teaspoon dried basil

½ teaspoon kosher salt

¼ teaspoon freshly ground pepper

2 large eggs, beaten, divided

1 cup Homestyle Breadcrumbs (see page 146)

Olive oil cooking spray

In a medium bowl, combine the ricotta, flour, thyme, rosemary, basil, salt, pepper, and half of the beaten eggs. Stir until well mixed.

Scoop approximately 1 tablespoon of the mixture into the palm of your hand and roll into a ball. Repeat with the remaining mixture.

Dip each of the balls into the remaining beaten egg and then into the breadcrumbs, coating evenly.

Place the balls on a cookie sheet, and refrigerate for 1 hour.

Spray the ricotta balls with olive oil cooking spray before adding to the basket, being careful not to overcrowd it. Air fry in batches at 400°F until golden, about 8–9 minutes.

PARMESAN GARLIC KNOTS

SERVES 10–12

Three dozen garlic knots is plenty for a party, right? Maybe not. These addictive little bites will go fast, especially if you serve them up with Marinara Dipping Sauce (see page 131).

1 (13.8-ounce) refrigerated pizza crust

3 tablespoons olive oil

3 tablespoons minced garlic

Garlic salt, for dusting

Grated Parmesan cheese, for dusting

Spread the pizza crust onto a cutting board. Cut it in half lengthwise, then cut each half into ¼-inch vertical strips (so that the strips are short, not long). Tie each strip into a knot.

Combine the oil and garlic in a small bowl, and dip the knots into the mixture one at a time, placing the dipped knots back onto the cutting board.

Once you have dipped all the knots, sprinkle garlic salt over the top of them.

Transfer the knots to the air fryer basket, and air fry in batches of 12 or so at 400°F for 4 minutes, checking for doneness halfway through the cooking time. The knots should be browned.

Once cooked, top the knots with a dusting of Parmesan cheese and serve hot.

Skinny Cauliflower Croquettes

SKINNY CAULIFLOWER CROQUETTES

SERVES 3–4

Your guests will never know that these yummy croquettes are on the lighter side of fried appetizers. Boiling the cauliflower gives it the same creamy consistency as potatoes, and Parmesan adds flavor with fewer calories than Cheddar or other cheeses.

2 cups cauliflower florets

1 cup Panko Breadcrumbs (see page 147)

¼ cup freshly grated Parmesan cheese

1 large egg, beaten

Olive oil cooking spray

Blanch the cauliflower by heating it in boiling water for 2–3 minutes, then immediately rinsing it with cold water to stop the cooking process. Place it in a bowl and let it cool for 5 minutes.

Toss the breadcrumbs with the Parmesan cheese.

Dip each of the florets into the beaten egg, then into the breadcrumb mixture, coating evenly.

Place the florets into the basket of the air fryer, leaving space around each one. Spray with olive oil cooking spray, then place the basket into the air fryer.

Air fry in batches at 400°F until golden, about 10 minutes.

BUFFALO CAULIFLOWER

SERVES 4

This vegetarian alternative to Buffalo wings gives you all the heat without the meat. Air frying the florets creates a nice crunch on the outside while keeping them creamy on the inside.

¼ cup melted butter

¼ cup hot sauce

1 cup Panko Breadcrumbs (see page 147)

1 teaspoon kosher salt

4 cups medium cauliflower florets

In a small bowl, combine the melted butter with the hot sauce. In another small bowl, combine the breadcrumbs and salt.

Dip the head of each floret into the sauce to coat, then dredge in the breadcrumb mixture.

Place the crumbed florets in the basket, and air fry at 350°F for 14–17 minutes until browned, shaking the basket 2 or 3 times during cooking to flip the cauliflower.

SWEET CORN FRITTERS

SERVES 3–4

If you're lucky enough to have farmer's markets by you, Sweet Corn Fritters are a great way to take advantage of all that fresh summer corn that suddenly surrounds you (though frozen corn will work in a pinch). Making these corn fritters in the air fryer ensures a crispy outer shell and soft inner cake.

1 tablespoon olive oil

2 shallots, finely chopped

2 cups corn kernels

1 large egg, beaten

½ cup 2% milk

2 tablespoons butter, melted

½ cup freshly grated Parmesan cheese

½ cup cornmeal

½ cup all-purpose flour

½ teaspoon kosher salt

¼ teaspoon freshly ground black pepper

Canola oil cooking spray

In a saucepan, heat the olive oil over medium heat, then add the shallots. Sauté until soft, approximately 2–3 minutes, stirring occasionally.

Add the corn and toss together, sautéing an additional 1–2 minutes. Remove from heat and set aside.

In a large mixing bowl, combine the egg, milk, butter, and Parmesan cheese. Then add the corn-shallots mixture, cornmeal, flour, salt, and pepper. Toss well to combine and let sit for 10–15 minutes to thicken.

Scoop approximately 2 tablespoons of the mixture into the palm of your hand and shape into either a ball or pancake, depending on your preference. Repeat until you use up the remaining mixture.

Spray the fritters with canola oil cooking spray and add them to the basket. Be sure not to overcrowd the basket or allow the fritters to touch each other.

Air fry in batches at 400°F until golden, about 10 minutes.

ZUCCHINI CAKES

SERVES 2–3

You may have had zucchini before, but you've never had zucchini like this. Parmesan cheese, garlic, and scallions pack in the flavor while the air fryer creates the perfect crunch. Serve them with some Sriracha Aioli (see page 129) for a little kick.

1 medium zucchini, peeled and grated

¼ cup freshly grated Parmesan cheese

1 large egg, beaten

½ teaspoon kosher salt

¼ teaspoon freshly ground black pepper

1 garlic clove, minced

1 large scallion, white and green parts, finely chopped

½ cup Italian Breadcrumbs (see page 146)

Olive oil cooking spray

In a medium bowl, combine the zucchini, Parmesan, egg, salt, and pepper, and mix until combined. Mix in the garlic and chopped scallion, then fold in the breadcrumbs.

Scoop about 2 tablespoons of the mixture into the palm of your hand. Roll into a ball and then flatten into a pancake, about ¼-inch thick. Repeat with remaining mixture.

Place the fritters in the basket of the air fryer, leaving space around each one. Spray on all sides with olive oil cooking spray.

Air fry at 390°F until golden, about 7 minutes.

STUFFED JALAPEÑOS

SERVES 4

While some recipes make you choose, this take on jalapeño poppers has the best of both cheesy worlds—cream cheese and Cheddar. Coat the peppers in your own homemade breadcrumbs (stem on, for a built-in "handle"), and pop them in the air fryer for a super easy and flavorful addition to any party.

1 (8-ounce) package cream cheese, softened

1 cup shredded Cheddar cheese

2 tablespoons fresh cilantro, chopped

1 tablespoon chipotle or other hot sauce

24 small jalapeño chilies, cut in half lengthwise and seeded

2 large eggs, beaten

1 cup Homestyle Breadcrumbs (see page 146)

Olive or canola oil cooking spray

Kosher salt and freshly ground black pepper, to taste

In a large bowl, mix together the cream cheese, Cheddar cheese, cilantro, and hot sauce.

Spoon the cheese and cilantro mixture into 1 jalapeño half, and top with an empty half. Push the halves together; the cream cheese will act as a glue. Repeat the process with the rest of the jalapeños.

Dip each of the peppers into the beaten egg and then into the breadcrumbs, coating evenly.

When all the peppers have been coated, refrigerate them for at least 1 hour and as long as overnight.

Spray the peppers with oil and place the first batch in the cooking basket. Season them with salt and pepper. Air fry in batches at 400°F until golden brown, about 12 minutes.

CRISPY MASHED POTATO BALLS

SERVES 4

A little egg yolk and flour turn boring mashed potatoes into something much better—crispy twice-baked potato croquettes. Although this is a great way to use up leftovers, the mashed potato recipe below has a cheesy flavor boost you might like better.

MASHED POTATOES

2 medium russet potatoes, peeled and cubed

1 tablespoon unsalted butter

¼ cup whole milk

¼ teaspoon kosher salt

½ cup freshly grated Parmesan cheese

CROQUETTES

Yolk of 1 large egg

2 tablespoons all-purpose our, plus extra for rolling

2 tablespoons finely chopped fresh chives

⅛ teaspoon freshly ground black pepper

Mashed potatoes

2 large eggs, beaten

½ cup Panko Breadcrumbs (see page 147)

Olive oil cooking spray

TO MAKE THE MASHED POTATOES:

Boil the potatoes in salted water until soft, about 15 minutes. Drain.

Add the butter, milk, salt, and Parmesan cheese. Using a masher, ricer, or fork, mash the potatoes just until well blended, and there are minimal lumps. Set aside to cool.

TO MAKE THE CROQUETTES:

Add the egg yolk, flour, chives, and pepper to the cooled potatoes.

Scoop out approximately 1 tablespoon of the mixture and roll it into a ball shape. Repeat with the remaining mixture.

Roll each croquette in flour to coat, dip into the beaten egg, and then roll into the breadcrumbs, coating evenly.

Spray each ball with cooking spray before adding it to the basket. Air fry (in batches if necessary) at 390°F for 8 minutes, or until golden.

GUILT-FREE VEGGIE SPRING ROLLS

SERVES 4

Between the Asian Ginger Spring Rolls (see page 23) and these lighter bites, your guests are covered! Serve up the Guilt-Free Veggie Spring Rolls with Thai Sweet Chili Sauce (see page 134) for a delicious duo.

1 cup thinly sliced cabbage

¼ cup coarsely grated carrot

¼ cup chopped green onion

1 tablespoon soy sauce

2 tablespoons sesame seeds

8 spring roll wrappers

¼ cup water

2 tablespoons olive oil

In a medium bowl, mix together the first 5 ingredients.

Place the wrappers on a clean, dry surface. Spoon the mixture evenly into each wrapper near the bottom corner. Lift this corner up on each wrapper, and roll until you use up half of the wrapper. Fold the sides in, then continue rolling, tucking the edges in as you go, until finished.

Dab a small amount of water onto the remaining corner with your fingertip, then press it against the spring roll to seal. Repeat with the remaining wrappers and filling.

Brush the spring rolls with a light coating of olive oil and place them in the basket seam-side down, leaving space between them. Air fry at 375°F for about 5–8 minutes or until golden and crunchy.

ASIAN GINGER SPRING ROLLS

SERVES 4

These crunchy little rolls pack a big flavor punch with ginger, garlic, lime, and Asian sauces. Finish them off with a drizzle of Thai Sweet Chili Sauce (see page 134) for a starter that beats anything you'll find at a restaurant.

4 ounces boneless chicken breast, cooked and roughly chopped

1 celery stalk, roughly chopped

1 medium carrot, peeled and roughly chopped

1/2 cup chopped baby bella mushrooms

1/2 teaspoon freshly grated ginger

1 garlic clove, minced

1/4 teaspoon freshly ground black pepper

1 tablespoon soy sauce

1 tablespoon hoisin sauce

1 teaspoon lime juice

1 large egg

1 teaspoon cornstarch

8–10 refrigerated spring roll wrappers (or frozen spring roll wrappers, thawed)

Olive oil cooking spray

Place the chicken, celery, carrot, and mushrooms in a food processor, and pulse until shredded. Add the ginger, garlic, and pepper, and pulse until well mixed, about 1 minute. Stir in the soy sauce, hoisin sauce, and lime juice.

In a small bowl, whisk together the egg and the cornstarch. The resulting paste will become the glue that holds each wrapper together.

Place each wrapper on a clean, dry surface, with a corner facing you. Spoon approximately 1 tablespoon of the filling onto a wrapper, near the bottom corner. Then lift this corner up and roll until you use up half of the wrapper. Fold the sides in, then continue rolling, tucking the edges in as you go, until you use all of the wrapper.

Dab a small amount of the cornstarch-egg mixture onto the remaining corner with your fingertip, then press it against the rest of the spring roll to seal. Repeat with the remaining wrappers and filling.

Spray the spring rolls liberally with cooking spray and place them seam-side down in the cooking basket, leaving space around each one.

Air fry in batches at 390°F until golden and crunchy, about 6 minutes.

DUCK-FILLED CHINESE DUMPLINGS

SERVES 12–24

If you can't stand the side of grease that comes with takeout, you're going to love making dishes like these Duck-Filled Chinese Dumplings in your air fryer. You get all the flavor, and none of the grease!

1 stalk celery, chopped

¼ medium red onion, chopped

2 teaspoons freshly grated ginger

1½ tablespoons soy sauce

2 teaspoons sesame oil

1 teaspoon chili oil

1 tablespoon rice vinegar

3–4 ounces smoked duck breast

1 (12-ounce) package wonton skins

Olive oil cooking spray

In a food processor, combine all of the ingredients except the wonton skins and cooking spray. Pulse them into a fine paste.

Lay out the wonton skins on a clean work surface. Add about a teaspoon of the filling to the middle of each skin.

To fold the wontons: Using your fingertips, wet two edges of the wonton with a small amount of water, and then fold it over on the diagonal. Press the edges to seal it. Now pull up the two corners of the triangle and press to seal, forming a wonton shape. Repeat for rest of wontons.

Spray the air fryer basket and wontons with cooking spray. Air fry in batches at 390°F until crispy, about 6 minutes, shaking once during cooking time.

TEMPURA-STYLE VEGGIES

SERVES 4–6

Light-as-a-feather Japanese-style tempura batter lets these sweet veggies shine through for an appetizer that tastes better than freshly picked. Serve up your Tempura-Style Veggies with any of the sauces on pages 132–134.

½ cup cornstarch

½ cup all-purpose flour

1 large egg, lightly beaten

¾ cup cold soda water

1 small Japanese eggplant, sliced into ¼-inch discs

1 small sweet potato, sliced into ¼-inch discs

1 red pepper, seeded and sliced into ¼-inch-long strips

1 cup broccoli florets

1 cup Panko Breadcrumbs (see page 147)

Canola oil cooking spray

Kosher salt and freshly ground black pepper, to taste

In a large bowl, fold together the cornstarch, flour, egg, and soda water. The batter will be slightly lumpy. Let sit, covered, for 30 minutes.

Dip each vegetable into the batter, shaking off any excess. Then dredge in the breadcrumbs, pressing on each side to coat evenly.

Place the veggies in the basket with space around each one, and spray them on all sides with oil. Air fry in batches at 400°F until golden, about 7 minutes. Season with salt and pepper, and serve.

HOT WINGS FOR TWO

SERVES 2

It might not be the big game, but any game night isn't quite right without spicy Buffalo wings. Keep things from getting soggy by frying the wings first, then tossing them in the sauce.

6 bone-in chicken wings

4 tablespoons unsalted butter, melted

4 tablespoons hot sauce

1 teaspoon cider vinegar

1 teaspoon soy sauce

1 teaspoon ketchup

Rinse the wings, and pat them dry. Section the wings in three parts, discarding the tips. Place the midsections and drumettes in the basket, and air fry at 400°F until cooked through, about 25 minutes. Shake the basket 2 or 3 times during cooking to flip the wings.

While the chicken is cooking, prepare the sauce: In a large bowl, whisk together the melted butter, hot sauce, cider vinegar, soy sauce, and ketchup.

When the wings finish cooking, add them to bowl and toss with the sauce to coat.

HONEY SRIRACHA WINGS

SERVES 2

Who doesn't love a crunchy honey-hot wing? Making Honey Sriracha Wings in the air fryer means you get a perfectly crispy skin under the sauce. Cool these down with some Creamy Lime Dip (see page 136).

1 pound bone-in chicken wings

¼ cup honey

2 tablespoons sriracha sauce

1 tablespoon soy sauce

1 tablespoon butter

Juice of 1 lime

Rinse the wings, and pat them dry using a paper towel. Section the wings in three parts, discarding the tips. Place the midsections and drumettes in the basket, and air fry at 360°F until cooked through, about 30 minutes. Use tongs to flip the wings every 7 minutes or so.

While the chicken is cooking, prepare the sauce: Add the remaining ingredients to a small saucepan over medium heat, and bring to a boil. Cook for an additional 3 minutes.

When the wings finish cooking, toss them with the sauce to coat. Serve immediately.

Hot Wings for Two

SWEET ASIAN-STYLE WINGS

SERVES 2

If you like a little sweetness with your spice, these are the wings for you. Honey and brown sugar pair with garlic and ginger for a perfectly balanced blend of flavor—no blue cheese or celery required!

6 bone-in chicken wings

½ cup soy sauce

2 garlic cloves, minced

4 tablespoons fresh ginger, shredded

⅓ cup light brown sugar

⅓ cup honey

Freshly ground black pepper, to taste

3 tablespoons cornstarch

Rinse the wings, and pat them dry. Section the wings in three parts, discarding the tips. Place the midsections and drumettes in the basket and air fry at 400°F until cooked through, about 25 minutes. Shake the basket 2 or 3 times during cooking to flip the wings.

While the wings are cooking, prepare the sauce: In a medium saucepan, over medium heat, mix together the soy sauce, garlic, ginger, brown sugar, honey, and pepper, stirring continuously.

As the sugar melts and the honey thins, begin adding the cornstarch a pinch at a time. Keep stirring in the cornstarch until you arrive at the desired consistency for your sauce, then remove it from heat.

When the wings are done cooking, place them in a large bowl. Pour the sauce over the wings and toss to coat.

CHAPTER TWO
DELICIOUS MEALS:
BREAKFAST, LUNCH, & DINNER

BLUEBERRY MUFFINS

SERVES 4

These light-as-air muffins, dotted with fresh blueberries, are a refreshing way to start your day. Don't worry—you won't miss the muffin tin. Just double up on each muffin's paper cup to keep its contents intact.

⅔ cup all-purpose flour

1½ teaspoons baking powder

3 tablespoons granulated sugar

1 pinch of kosher salt

1 large egg

½ teaspoon vanilla

⅓ cup 2% or whole milk

3 tablespoons unsalted butter, melted

½ cup fresh blueberries

In a large bowl, mix together the flour, baking powder, sugar, and salt.

In a medium bowl, whisk together the egg, vanilla, and milk, then add the melted butter. Stir well to combine.

Add the wet mixture to the flour mixture, and whisk just until lumps disappear. Gently fold in the blueberries.

Place 4 doubled-up muffin cups into the air fryer basket and carefully spoon the batter into the cups, filling them ¾ full.

Air fry at 320°F until a toothpick inserted into the center of a muffin comes out clean, about 15–20 minutes.

PERFECT PUMPKIN MUFFINS

SERVES 12

Calling all pumpkin lovers! High in both fiber and flavor, these healthy pumpkin muffins will keep you full and energized for hours.

1 cup pumpkin purée

2 cups oats

½ cup honey

2 medium eggs, beaten

1 teaspoon coconut butter

1 tablespoon vanilla

1 teaspoon nutmeg

Add all of the ingredients to a food processor, and mix them on low until smooth. Divide the mixture evenly between 12 doubled-up paper muffin cups.

Air fry at 355°F in batches for about 15 minutes or until a toothpick inserted in the center of the muffins comes out clean. Let cool and serve.

FRENCH TOAST STICKS

SERVES 2

If you're craving something a little bit sweet for breakfast, these sticks are a healthy compromise— especially if you top them off with fresh fruit. For a little extra flavor, use store-bought bread made with cinnamon.

2 large eggs

¼ cup 2% milk

¼ cup brown sugar

1 tablespoon honey

1 teaspoon cinnamon

⅛ teaspoon nutmeg

4 slices whole grain bread

Powdered sugar, for dusting

In a medium bowl, combine all of the ingredients except the bread and powdered sugar.

Cut the slices of bread into 4 sections (or sticks) each. Dip the bread sections in the wet mixture to coat evenly, transferring each to the air fryer basket.

Air fry at 320°F for 10 minutes, flipping once, until sections are browned and crisp. Top with a dusting of powdered sugar.

VANILLA-GLAZED DOUGHNUTS

SERVES 10–12

It doesn't get more decadent than doughnuts, but without all of the oil used in traditional frying, you get to enjoy these light and fluffy wonders without the usual side of guilt. You'll need to leave lots of time for the dough to rise, so plan accordingly. If you want a quicker route, use a refrigerated tin of biscuits from the store instead—the doughnuts will taste just as amazing!

GLAZE

1½ cups powdered sugar

2 tablespoons whole milk

2 teaspoons pure vanilla extract

DOUGHNUTS

1¼ cups milk, warmed

¼ cup granulated sugar

1 (.25-ounce) packet active dry yeast

2 large eggs, beaten

1 stick unsalted butter, melted

1 teaspoon salt

4¼ cups all-purpose flour, plus more if needed

Canola oil cooking spray

TO MAKE THE GLAZE:

Combine all of the glaze ingredients in a bowl, and stir until smooth. Set aside.

TO MAKE THE DOUGHNUTS:

In a medium bowl, combine the warm milk and sugar, and mix until the sugar dissolves. Then add the yeast and let the mixture sit until it starts to bubble, 5–10 minutes.

In a separate medium bowl, whisk together the eggs and the melted butter.

In the bowl of an electric stand mixer fitted with a dough hook attachment, combine the egg-butter mixture, the milk mixture, and the salt. Mix on low speed until well combined, about 1 minute.

While continuing to mix on low speed, add the flour 1 cup at a time to the mixer bowl, allowing each cup to be absorbed before adding the next cup.

Continue mixing until the dough begins to pull away from the sides of the bowl, about 5 minutes after the flour is fully combined. If the dough is too wet, add more flour 1 tablespoon at a time.

Place the dough in a lightly greased bowl, then cover and refrigerate it overnight (at least 8 hours).

Remove the dough from the refrigerator, and place it in a warm location to rise for 2 hours.

Turn the dough out onto a floured work surface, and roll it with a rolling pin until it is about ¼-inch thick. Cut it into 1-inch rounds with a biscuit cutter, cookie cutter, or drinking glass, and then cut a hole in the center of each with a smaller cookie cutter or shot glass.

Place each doughnut on a parchment-lined baking sheet. Cover them with clean kitchen towels, and return the sheet to a warm location to let the dough rise for 2 more hours.

Place the doughnuts in the basket of the air fryer, making sure to leave space around each one. Spray them on both sides with canola oil.

Air fry in batches at 400°F until golden, about 5 minutes, flipping them halfway through the cooking time. As soon as the doughnuts are cool enough to touch, dip each in the glaze.

PERSONAL PAN FRITTATA

SERVES 1

This simple frittata is a great way to start your day on the right foot when all you want is your coffee cup. In less than 10 minutes—start to finish—you'll have a healthy, filling, and delicious breakfast you can actually sink your teeth into.

2 large eggs

1 tablespoon freshly grated Parmesan cheese

2 tablespoons 2% milk

⅛ teaspoon kosher salt

⅛ teaspoon freshly ground black pepper

Canola oil cooking spray

¼ cup baby spinach, roughly chopped

2 cherry tomatoes, sliced

In a medium bowl, whisk together the eggs, Parmesan cheese, milk, salt, and pepper.

Spray an air fryer baking pan with canola oil and place it in the basket. Pour the egg mixture into the pan, and then delicately fold in the spinach and tomatoes.

Air fry at 400°F until cooked through, about 5 minutes. Serve warm.

EGG WHITE FRITTATA

SERVES 2

If you like to keep your breakfast light, Egg White Frittata is for you. Mushrooms and tomatoes are the stars of the Egg White Frittata, but feel free to add or substitute your favorite veggies.

1 cup egg whites

2 tablespoons skim milk

¼ cup sliced tomato

¼ cup sliced mushrooms

2 tablespoons chopped fresh chives

Kosher salt and freshly ground black pepper, to taste

Olive oil cooking spray

Mix together all ingredients except the cooking spray in a medium bowl until well combined.

Spray an air fryer baking pan with the cooking spray, and place it in the air fryer basket. Transfer the mixture to the pan, and air fry at 320°F for 15 minutes or until the frittata is cooked through.

BACON, EGG, AND CHEESE SANDWICH

SERVES 1

If you're running late, you can still start your day with a savory, protein-packed breakfast. An English muffin toasts right alongside the bacon and egg in this quick and easy air fryer meal.

1 large egg

Kosher salt and freshly ground black pepper, to taste

2 slices bacon

1 English muffin, sliced in half

1 slice Cheddar cheese

Crack the egg into an ovenproof soufflé cup or bowl, and season with salt and pepper. Place the egg, bacon, and muffin slices in the air fryer basket, leaving space between them.

Air fry at 392°F for about 6 minutes, until the bacon is crisp and the egg is cooked through. Assemble the sandwich, including the cheese, and enjoy hot.

PERSONAL PIZZAS

SERVES 3–4

Did you know you could make deliciously crispy-crusted pizza in an air fryer? This version makes Margherita-style pizza, but feel free to add your favorite toppings. And if you're running short on time, just grab some refrigerated pizza dough from the grocery store.

DOUGH

1 (.25-ounce) packet active dry yeast

1/4 cup granulated sugar

1 2/3 cups warm (100°F–110°F) water, divided

3/4 cup extra virgin olive oil

1 tablespoon kosher salt

5 cups all-purpose flour, plus more for dusting

PIZZAS

1 (28-ounce) can whole peeled tomatoes, drained

2 tablespoons extra virgin olive oil

1/2 teaspoon dried oregano

1 teaspoon kosher salt

1/2 teaspoon freshly ground black pepper

6 ounces fresh mozzarella cheese, torn into 6 pieces

6–12 fresh basil leaves

TO MAKE THE DOUGH:

In a medium bowl, combine the yeast, sugar, and 1 cup of the water. Stir until the sugar dissolves.

Pour the mixture into the bowl of an electric stand mixer fit with a dough hook attachment. Add the remaining water, olive oil, and salt. Add the flour, and beat at low speed until dough comes together and is smooth, about 10 minutes.

Cover the bowl of dough with lightly greased plastic wrap, and let it rise in a warm place free from drafts until it doubles in bulk, about 1 1/2 hours.

Punch down the dough, and turn it out onto a lightly floured surface. Divide it into 6 portions for individual pizzas. For each pizza, place a dough round in the pizza pan and fold any excess inward, pressing it into the crust.

TO MAKE THE PIZZAS:

In a large bowl, crush the tomatoes repeatedly with your hands until they reach your desired consistency. Stir in the olive oil, oregano, salt, and pepper.

Spread the tomato mixture over each dough round, leaving a border around the edge. Top each with 1 ounce of the mozzarella cheese.

Air fry in batches at 400°F until the crust is golden brown and the cheese is melted, about 10 minutes. Garnish each pie with 1 or 2 basil leaves.

PORTOBELLO PIZZAS

SERVES 4

Forego the flour and the calories, and discover pizza in a new light. Here, we're air frying portobello mushrooms packed with tomatoes, spinach, garlic, and cheese for a dish that's as hearty as it is healthy.

8 ounces fresh spinach

1 garlic clove, minced

4 tablespoons olive oil, divided

2 medium tomatoes, diced

½ cup fresh basil, chopped

Kosher salt and freshly ground black pepper, to taste

1 tablespoon red wine vinegar

4 large portobello mushrooms, stems and gills removed

½ cup Parmesan cheese, grated

1½ cups mozzarella cheese, grated

In a small pan, sauté the spinach with the garlic and 2 tablespoons of the olive oil over low heat until it's wilted. Set it aside.

Combine the tomatoes, basil, salt, pepper, remaining 2 tablespoons of olive oil, and red wine vinegar in a large bowl.

Divide the tomato-basil mixture into the portobello caps. Top each with the sautéed spinach, followed by the Parmesan and mozzarella cheeses.

Air fry at 380°F until the mushrooms are tender and the cheese begins to brown, about 6 minutes.

CRISPY EGGPLANT PARM

SERVES 4

Eggplant Parmesan is an Italian classic for a reason—vegetables, cheese, breadcrumbs, and sauce have never come together so perfectly. In this version, using eggplant as vessels for the ingredients creates a deliciously tidy little dish.

2 small eggplants

¼ cup extra virgin olive oil

1 teaspoon kosher salt

½ teaspoon freshly ground black pepper

1 cup Italian Breadcrumbs (see page 146)

1 cup Marinara Dipping Sauce (see page 131)

8 slices fresh mozzarella cheese

½ cup freshly grated Parmesan cheese

¼ cup chopped fresh basil

Rinse the eggplants and pat them dry. Do not peel them, but slice off the tops, and then slice each eggplant in half lengthwise.

Coat the outside of each eggplant half with olive oil, and season it with salt and pepper. Sprinkle a ¼ cup of the breadcrumbs onto each section.

Line the pan of your air fryer with aluminum foil. Place the eggplant halves in the pan, leaving space around each one, and air fry in batches at 390°F for 10 minutes.

Remove the eggplant from the air fryer, and top each half (cut-side up) with an even helping of Marinara Dipping Sauce and 2 slices of mozzarella (cut the slices in half to more efficiently cover the eggplant, if desired). Sprinkle each half with Parmesan cheese.

Place the eggplant back inside the air fryer until the cheese melts, an additional 5–7 minutes. Sprinkle with the chopped basil.

ZESTY FALAFEL

SERVES 2–4

Can't get enough of the food cart outside of work? Try making one of those favorites at home. This vegetarian Middle Eastern dish cooks up beautifully in the air fryer and is chock full of healthy protein thanks to its main ingredient: chickpeas.

1 (8-ounce) can chickpeas

2 garlic cloves

1 small Spanish onion, quartered

½ tablespoon chopped fresh Italian flat-leaf parsley leaves

1 tablespoon chopped fresh cilantro leaves

¼ teaspoon kosher salt

1 pinch crushed red pepper flakes

2 tablespoons olive oil

¼ cup all-purpose flour

⅛ teaspoon baking powder

Canola oil cooking spray

Add all of the ingredients except the cooking spray to your food processor. Pulse until combined (it should be similar to the texture of cooked oatmeal), about 2–3 minutes. Cover and refrigerate for 1–2 hours.

Scoop approximately 2 tablespoons of the mixture into the palm of your hand, and shape into a ball. Repeat with remaining mixture.

Spray the falafel balls with canola oil cooking spray, and place them in the basket, leaving space around each one. Air fry in batches at 390°F until golden, about 10 minutes.

CHICKEN FAJITAS

SERVES 2

When your mouth is watering for fresh Mexican food, this Chicken Fajitas recipe is a must-try! You'll find both seasoned and unseasoned chicken fajita strips in the freezer aisle, so it's easy to customize the flavors of the dish to your liking. Top things off with the cool and complementary Creamy Lime Dip on page 136.

Olive oil cooking spray

2 large (10-inch) flour tortillas

½ cup shredded Mexican four-cheese blend, divided

1 cup packaged chicken fajita strips

½ cup sliced green and red peppers

½ cup sliced onion

Lightly spray the air fryer pan with olive oil, and place 1 tortilla inside.

Spread half of the cheese over the tortilla, and top with the chicken in a single layer. Sprinkle the slices of pepper and onion over the chicken, and top with the remaining cheese (adding more, if you prefer).

Top your fajita with the second tortilla, and spray it lightly with cooking spray. Place the air fryer rack on top of the fajita to keep it in place.

Air fry at 370°F for 4 minutes, flip the fajita using a spatula, and then air fry for 4 more minutes or until golden brown. Use a pizza cutter to quarter the fajita, and serve hot.

Brown Sugar Barbecue Chicken

BROWN SUGAR BARBECUE CHICKEN

SERVES 2–4

The air fryer makes quick work of weeknight dinners. In this one, brown sugar balances out balsamic vinegar for a scrumptiously smooth-tasting barbecue chicken. Whip up a side of some Sweet Potato Fries (see page 111), and you'll have one very tasty plate!

5 tablespoons balsamic vinegar

5 tablespoons brown sugar

3 tablespoons extra virgin olive oil

2 teaspoons Dijon mustard

2 garlic cloves, minced

1 tablespoon finely chopped onion

Kosher salt and freshly ground black pepper, to taste

4 boneless, skinless chicken thighs

In a large bowl, mix together all ingredients except the chicken. Let the mixture sit, covered, for at least 1 hour.

After 1 hour, add the chicken to the sauce and toss well to coat thoroughly.

Place the chicken on the air fryer rack, leaving space around each piece. Air fry in batches at 380°F until cooked through, about 15 minutes.

BETTER FRIED CHICKEN FINGERS

SERVES 2

Just a bit of seasoning and crispy breadcrumbs are all you need to make a great main dish. Even the pickiest little ones will love this healthier take on chicken tenders!

12 ounces of chicken breasts

Kosher salt and freshly ground black pepper, to taste

⅛ cup flour

1 egg white, beaten

½ cup Panko Breadcrumbs (see page 147)

Olive oil cooking spray

Trim the chicken of any excess fat, and slice it into six tenders. Season each with salt and pepper.

Dredge each strip in the flour, coating each side. Dip into the beaten egg, and then press each side into the breadcrumbs, coating evenly.

Transfer the tenders to the basket, spray them with olive oil, and air fry them at 350°F for about 10 minutes.

BUTTERMILK FRIED CHICKEN

SERVES 4–6

This Southern-style chicken is better than you'll find at any fast-food window. Crispy on the outside, tender on the inside, and spiced to perfection, Buttermilk Fried Chicken will become an instant family favorite. Serve it with any of the sauces on pages 128–129.

1 tablespoon garlic powder

1 tablespoon sweet paprika

1 tablespoon chili powder

1/2–1 tablespoon cayenne pepper

1 1/2 tablespoons kosher salt, divided

1 tablespoon + 1 teaspoon freshly ground black pepper, divided

10 pieces of chicken (thighs, split breasts, wings, or drumsticks)

3 large eggs

3/4 cup buttermilk

1/4 cup water

1 cup all-purpose flour

1 cup cornstarch

2 cups Homestyle Breadcrumbs (see page 146)

Canola oil cooking spray

In a large bowl, combine the garlic powder, paprika, chili powder, cayenne pepper, and 1 tablespoon each of the salt and pepper. Add the chicken pieces and toss to coat. Cover and refrigerate overnight.

In a shallow bowl, beat together the eggs, buttermilk, and water.

In a separate shallow bowl, combine the flour, cornstarch, the remaining 1/2 tablespoon of salt, and 1 teaspoon of pepper. Put the breadcrumbs in another shallow bowl.

Dip each piece of the chicken into the flour mixture, then the buttermilk mixture, and then the breadcrumbs. Spray on all sides with canola oil. Place the chicken in the air fryer basket, leaving room around each piece.

Air fry in batches at 370°F until cooked through and crispy, about 25 minutes, flipping halfway through the cooking time.

SPICY PECAN-CRUSTED CHICKEN FINGERS

SERVES 2–4

If your family likes a little heat with their fried chicken, Spicy Pecan-Crusted Chicken Fingers is the recipe for you. Adding pecans to the breadcrumb mixture and air frying the chicken makes it mouthwateringly tender inside and crunchy outside.

½ cup pecans

¼ cup Panko or Homestyle Breadcrumbs (see pages 146–147)

Zest of 1 orange

½ teaspoon kosher salt

1 large egg

1 tablespoon sauce from a can of chipotle chili peppers in adobo

1 pound white-meat chicken, sliced into strips

1 cup flour

Canola oil cooking spray

In a food processor, combine the pecans, breadcrumbs, orange zest, and salt. Pulse until fine.

In a separate bowl, whisk together the egg and adobo sauce.

Dip each of the chicken pieces into the flour and then the egg mixture. Then press each side into the pecan-chipotle mixture to coat evenly.

Place the chicken fingers in the basket, leaving space around each one, and spray on all sides with canola oil.

Air fry in batches at 400°F until golden, about 13 minutes, flipping halfway through the cooking time.

THAI-STYLE CHICKEN SKEWERS

SERVES 4

Prepare this sweet-and-savory recipe the night before you need it for a quick and easy weeknight meal. While grilling chicken satay is traditional, it can result in a dry dish. Air frying ensures moist and delicious chicken every time.

3 tablespoons freshly ground or natural-style peanut butter

½ cup soy sauce

½ cup pineapple juice

2 garlic cloves, minced

1 tablespoon freshly grated ginger

1 pound boneless, skinless chicken breasts or tenderloins, pounded to ¼-inch thickness

4 skewers

In a large bowl, combine the first five ingredients and whisk until smooth. Add the chicken and toss well to thoroughly coat. Cover and refrigerate for at least 2 hours, but preferably overnight.

Remove the chicken from the marinade, and blot the excess marinade with a paper towel. Thread the chicken onto skewers, and place them into the air fryer basket, leaving space around each one.

Air fry in batches at 400°F until cooked through, about 10 minutes. Serve with Thai-Style Peanut Sauce (see page 133).

HONEY-SESAME CHICKEN KEBABS

SERVE 2

Chicken and veggies smothered in honeyed soy sauce make a scrumptious and satisfying light meal. Choose your favorite variety of bell pepper, or cut up a few for more colorful kebabs.

⅓ cup honey

⅓ cup soy sauce

1 teaspoon sesame seeds

Kosher salt and freshly ground pepper, to taste

2 chicken breasts, diced into 1-inch cubes

1 bell pepper, cut into 1-inch squares

6 white button mushrooms, halved

5 short skewers

In a medium bowl, combine the honey, soy sauce, sesame seeds, salt, and pepper. Toss the diced chicken in the mixture to coat.

Thread the chicken, peppers, and mushrooms onto the skewers in whatever pattern you like.

Place the kebabs in the air fryer, brush them with some of the remaining sauce mixture, and air fry at 338°F for 15–20 minutes or until chicken is cooked through. Garnish with additional sesame seeds, and serve.

MOROCCAN CHICKEN

SERVES 2–4

Exotic, aromatic, and delicious, Moroccan Chicken will cause serious cravings. The spice mix is like no dry rub you've ever tasted, so you'll want to save any leftover mix for another mouthwatering batch.

SPICE RUB

3 tablespoons smoked paprika

1 tablespoon crushed red pepper

1 tablespoon ground ginger

2 teaspoons cumin seeds

1 teaspoon ground turmeric

1 teaspoon kosher salt

1 teaspoon fenugreek seeds

1 teaspoon coriander seeds

1 teaspoon ground cardamom

½ teaspoon ground cinnamon

½ teaspoon whole allspice

½ teaspoon black peppercorns

8 whole cloves

CHICKEN

4 boneless, skinless chicken thighs

Canola oil cooking spray

TO MAKE THE SPICE RUB:

Warm a small saucepan over medium-high heat and add all of the spice rub ingredients. Toast the spices, stirring constantly for approximately 1–2 minutes. Remove from heat as soon as they start to toast (they will become nutty and aromatic)—being careful not to burn them.

Pour the mixture into a bowl, and allow to cool for 10–15 minutes. Once cool, place it in a food processor and pulse until fine, about 1 minute.

TO MAKE THE CHICKEN:

Coat each chicken thigh with about 2 teaspoons of the spice rub, rubbing the mixture into the chicken with your fingers.

Spray the chicken pieces on all sides with canola oil, and then place on a rack in the air fryer. Air fry at 380°F until cooked through, about 25–30 minutes. Flip halfway through the cooking time.

CHINESE FIVE-SPICE DUCK

SERVES 2

Duck is a meaty, flavorful fowl made for Asian seasonings. If you're not in the mood to make your own Chinese five-spice mix, just pick up a packaged one at the store. This dish goes great with a mixed-greens salad topped off with Sesame-Ginger Dressing (see page 133).

3 tablespoons cinnamon

2 teaspoons anise seeds

1½ teaspoons fennel seeds

¾ teaspoon ground cloves

1 teaspoon kosher salt

1½ teaspoons freshly ground black pepper

2 duck legs

1 teaspoon chopped Thai basil

In a small bowl, combine the cinnamon, anise, fennel, cloves, salt, and pepper.

Rinse the duck legs, and pat them dry. Trim off any excess fat that hangs over the edge of the meat, and use a paring knife to cut several small slits in the skin and fat on the surface of the leg.

Coat the legs with the spice rub, rubbing it into the meat with your fingers.

Air fry at 340°F for 30 minutes, then increase the temperature to 400°F and continue air frying until the meat is cooked through and skin is crispy, about 5 minutes more. If necessary, drain off excess fat into a glass jar or aluminum can midway through the cooking process. Sprinkle with the basil before serving.

FAMILY FAVORITE PORK CHOPS

SERVES 4

While air-fried pork chops are yummy enough, garlic powder and seasoned breadcrumbs give these no-fuss cuts a delicious flavor boost. Serve up Family Favorite Pork Chops with Garlic Parmesan Potatoes (see page 106) for a dinner your entire family will love.

4 pork loin chops

1 teaspoon kosher salt

1 teaspoon freshly ground black pepper

1 cup Italian Breadcrumbs (see page 146)

1 tablespoon garlic powder

1 cup flour

1 large egg, beaten

Olive oil cooking spray

Rinse the pork chops, and pat them dry with paper towels. Season with the salt and pepper.

In a shallow bowl, combine the breadcrumbs and garlic powder. Dip each pork chop into the flour and then the beaten egg, then dredge in the breadcrumb mixture, turning to coat evenly.

Spray the chops on all sides with olive oil, and place them in the basket.

Air fry in batches at 400°F for 10 minutes, then flip the chops, and continue to air fry until cooked through and golden, about 5 minutes.

BARBECUE RIBS

SERVES 2

Did you know you can make melt-in-your-mouth sauce-covered ribs in your air fryer? This version even doubles up on flavor by using both a rub and a sauce.

RUB

1 tablespoon chili powder

1 tablespoon cumin

1 teaspoon garlic powder

1 teaspoon ground mustard

2 tablespoons kosher salt

1 teaspoon freshly ground black pepper

1 tablespoon dark brown sugar

RIBS

1 rack baby back ribs

½ cup red wine vinegar

SAUCE

3 tablespoons tomato sauce

2 tablespoons balsamic vinegar

2 tablespoons dark brown sugar

1 tablespoon mustard

1 tablespoon garlic powder

1 tablespoon kosher salt

TO MAKE THE RUB:

In a large bowl, combine all of the rub ingredients, and mix well. Set aside.

TO MAKE THE RIBS:

Rinse the rack, and pat it dry. With a sharp knife, slice the rack into ribs.

Pour the red wine vinegar into a bowl. Toss the ribs in the vinegar, then add the ribs to the bowl containing the rub. Rub the spice mixture into the meat with your fingers.

Stand the ribs up in the basket, and air fry them at 360°F for 30 minutes.

TO MAKE THE SAUCE:

Meanwhile, in a small saucepan, combine all of the sauce ingredients and heat over medium-low heat, stirring continuously, until the sugar dissolves, 3–5 minutes.

Remove the ribs from the air fryer. Brush the sauce onto the cooked ribs, and return the ribs to the air fryer for 5 minutes, or until sauce is bubbly and ribs are tender.

HONEY MUSTARD PORK

SERVES 4

With just a few ingredients, you can create a simple glaze that packs a big punch and transforms boring pork tenderloin into something amazing.

1 pound pork tenderloin, sliced into 1-inch-thick rounds

2 teaspoons kosher salt

1½ teaspoons freshly ground black pepper

2 tablespoons honey

2 tablespoons Dijon mustard

4 tablespoons water

2 teaspoons ground ginger

3 garlic cloves, crushed

1 pinch cayenne pepper

1 cup Homestyle Breadcrumbs (see page 146)

Season both sides of the pork rounds with the salt and pepper.

In a shallow bowl, combine the honey, mustard, water, ginger, garlic, and cayenne pepper, and mix well.

Dip each pork round into the honey-Dijon mixture, and then press each side into the breadcrumbs, coating evenly.

Place the rounds in the basket of the air fryer, leaving space around each one.

Air fry at 400°F for 10 minutes, then flip and air fry until golden brown, about 5 more minutes.

FRIED PORK WITH ASIAN DRESSING

SERVES 4

Pork and ginger are a perfect pair, and Fried Pork with Asian Dressing proves that. Topping tender air-fried pork with spinach, peppers, and homemade dressing means this scrumptious dish is also a healthy choice for the family.

1 tablespoon hot sauce

2 tablespoons light or dark brown sugar

1 garlic clove, minced

¼ teaspoon kosher salt

12 ounces pork tenderloin, trimmed and sliced crosswise into ½-inch thick slices

Canola oil cooking spray

3 cups baby spinach leaves

1 cup roughly chopped bell peppers (red, yellow, and orange)

¼ cup chopped fresh chives

In a large bowl, combine the hot sauce, brown sugar, garlic, and salt, and mix well to thoroughly combine. Add the pork slices and toss to coat. Let marinate at room temperature for at least 1 hour.

Remove the pork from the marinade, shaking off any excess, and place it in the basket. Spray each piece on all sides with canola oil. Air fry at 400°F until cooked through, about 10 minutes, flipping them halfway through the cooking time.

Toss the spinach with the peppers and chives, along with the Sesame-Ginger Dressing (see page 133). Serve it atop the pork.

LAMB POCKETS

SERVES 2–4

These savory little bites are a modern spin on classic meat pie. They pack a lot of flavor into a tiny package, making them as great an appetizer as they are a main dish. Spice them up by serving them with Fiery Cucumber Sauce (see page 141).

1 tablespoon olive oil

1 large shallot, finely chopped

1 garlic clove, minced

1 teaspoon crushed dried rosemary

1 pound ground lamb

Kosher salt and freshly ground black pepper, to taste

1 tablespoon fresh lemon juice

1 sheet refrigerated or frozen puff pastry, thawed

1 large egg, beaten and divided

Heat the olive oil in a saucepan over medium heat. Add the shallots and cook, stirring occasionally, about 2 minutes. Add the garlic and rosemary, and stir until the shallots and garlic are soft, about 30 seconds more.

Add the ground lamb, and stir to mix with the other ingredients. Cook until browned, stirring occasionally, about 10 minutes.

Remove the mixture from the heat and drain it. Add the salt, pepper, and lemon juice, and stir to combine. Set this aside to cool.

While the lamb is cooling, lay out the sheet of puff pastry dough. Using a 3-inch biscuit cutter, cut circles into the pastry.

Spoon approximately 1 tablespoon of the lamb mixture onto the bottom half of each dough circle, leaving a 1/8-inch border. For each pocket, apply some of the beaten egg to the bottom edge using the tip of your finger or a brush, then fold over the top half of the dough circle. Press the edges together with the tines of a fork.

Cover the pockets with plastic wrap, and refrigerate them for 20 minutes.

When you're ready for frying, place the pockets in the cooking basket, leaving space around each one. Brush them evenly with the remaining egg.

Air fry at 390°F until golden brown and crispy, about 12 minutes.

MOUTHWATERING MEATBALLS

SERVES 4–5

Air-fried meatballs are surprisingly crunchy outside while still being mouthwateringly moist inside. Throw these in a roll and top them with provolone cheese and some Marinara Dipping Sauce (see page 131), and you've got yourself one heck of a meatball sub.

1 pound ground chuck

1 small onion, finely chopped

1 garlic clove, minced

1 large egg, beaten

¼ cup Panko Breadcrumbs (see page 147)

1 teaspoon grated ginger

½ teaspoon ground cumin

½ teaspoon chili powder

1 teaspoon salt

¼ teaspoon freshly ground black pepper

Olive oil, to coat

In a large bowl, loosely mix together all of the ingredients, except the olive oil, using your hands.

Scoop approximately 3 tablespoons of the mixture into the palm of your hand, and roll it into a ball. Repeat with the remaining mixture.

Brush the meatballs on all sides with olive oil, and place them in the basket, leaving room around each one.

Air fry in batches at 400°F until cooked through and golden, about 12 minutes. Shake the basket once or twice during the cooking time to flip the meatballs.

INSIDE-OUT BURGERS

SERVES 2

Whether you serve up these burgers on buns or just enjoy them with a knife and fork, you may never go back to grilling. Top them off with lettuce, tomatoes, and any of the yummy sauces on pages 128–129.

12 ounces (3/4 pound) lean ground beef

3 tablespoons minced onion

4 teaspoons ketchup

2 teaspoons yellow mustard

Kosher salt and freshly ground black pepper, to taste

4 slices of Cheddar cheese, crumbled

8 dill pickle slices

Add the ground beef, minced onion, ketchup, mustard, salt, and pepper to a large bowl, and mix well. Divide the mixture into four equal portions, and flatten each into a thin patty.

Divide the cheese and pickles between two of the patties, leaving the edge of each patty uncovered. Top these with the remaining two patties (one each), and press the edges together to seal with toppings inside.

Air fry at 370°F for 20 minutes, flipping the burgers once during cooking.

BUNLESS MUSHROOM BURGERS

SERVES 4

Portobello mushrooms, creamy cheese, and breadcrumbs come together to create a sandwich so amazing you'll never miss the bread. Try serving them with the perfectly complementary Creamy Red Pepper Dip on page 132.

1 tablespoon extra virgin olive oil

8 large portobello mushroom caps, stems and gills removed

4 ounces Muenster cheese, shredded

4 ounces sharp Cheddar cheese, shredded

1 cup all-purpose flour

2 large eggs, beaten

1 cup Panko Breadcrumbs (see page TK)

Olive oil cooking spray

Heat the olive oil in a large saucepan over medium-high heat. Add the mushroom caps, and sear on each side, about 4–5 minutes per side. Remove them from the pan, and blot them with paper towels to remove excess moisture.

Fill 1 mushroom cap with ¼ of the Muenster and Cheddar cheeses, then top each with an additional cap. Repeat with the remaining caps and cheese.

Dredge a mushroom stack in the flour, dip it into the beaten egg, and then dip into the breadcrumbs, coating evenly. Repeat with the remaining mushroom stacks, and spray all with olive oil cooking spray.

Place 1 or 2 mushroom stacks in the air fryer. Air fry at 380°F until the cheese is melted, about 6 minutes, flipping halfway through the cooking time. Repeat with the remaining mushroom stacks.

STUFFED BELL PEPPERS

SERVES 4

Stuffed peppers are a family favorite for a reason—they're easy to make, full of flavor, and cover most (and sometimes all) of the food groups. The recipe for Stuffed Bell Peppers uses red peppers, but you could easily use green, orange, or yellow instead.

4 medium red peppers, tops and seeds removed

2 teaspoons olive oil

1 medium onion, finely chopped

2 cloves garlic, minced

16 ounces lean ground beef

1 teaspoon kosher salt

1 teaspoon freshly ground black pepper

2 teaspoons Worcestershire sauce

1 cup tomato sauce, divided

8 ounces shredded Cheddar cheese, divided

Bring water to a boil in a large pot, add the peppers, and cook them for 3 minutes.

Add the oil, onion, and garlic to a pan and sauté over medium heat until the onions are translucent and the garlic is fragrant, about 3 minutes. Set aside to cool.

In a large bowl, combine the cooked vegetables, beef, salt, pepper, Worcestershire sauce, half of the tomato sauce, and half of the shredded cheese. Divide the mixture evenly to fill the peppers. Top the peppers with the remaining tomato sauce and cheese.

Transfer the peppers to the air fryer basket, and cook (in batches, if necessary) at 390°F for 15–20 minutes, until the peppers are tender. Check the beef to make sure it's cooked through.

MARINATED SKIRT STEAK

SERVES 4

Another wonderful make-ahead meal, this slightly sweet skirt steak goes great with a salad or any of the sides on pages 88–114. To make the most of this flavorful cut of meat, you'll want to marinate it overnight and let the vinegar tenderize it.

½ cup soy sauce

2 tablespoons balsamic vinegar

2 tablespoons extra virgin olive oil

½ cup light brown sugar

¼ teaspoon ground ginger

¼ teaspoon black pepper

1 garlic clove, minced

1 pound skirt steak, sliced into 4 sections

In a medium bowl, combine all of the ingredients except for the steak.

Place the steak in a resealable plastic bag, and pour the marinade over it, ensuring that all of the meat is covered. Press the air out of the bag before sealing it, then wrap it tightly around the steak. Refrigerate for at least 2 hours, but preferably overnight.

Remove the meat from the refrigerator, and let it sit at room temperature for at least 30 minutes before cooking. Remove the steak from the marinade, and pat it dry with paper towels.

Place 2 of the steak cuts in the basket. Air fry at 390°F for 10–12 minutes, depending on desired level of doneness. Repeat with additional steak cuts.

Let the steak sit for at least 15 minutes after removing it from the air fryer before you serve it.

COCONUT-CORNFLAKE SHRIMP

SERVES 4–6

Coconut and cornflake cereal complement the natural sweetness of shrimp, while the air fryer turns them both into a perfectly crunchy coating. Serve these up with the slightly tart Creamy Lime Dip (see page 136) to balance things out.

2 large eggs

1 tablespoon water

1 cup sweetened coconut flakes

2/3 cup crumbs from cornflakes cereal

1 teaspoon kosher salt

1 pound large shrimp, peeled and deveined, tails still attached

1 cup cornstarch

Olive oil cooking spray

In a shallow bowl, beat together the eggs and the water.

In a separate bowl, combine the coconut flakes, cornflake crumbs, and salt.

Dredge each piece of shrimp in the cornstarch, then dip in the egg, and then roll in the coconut-cornflake mixture, until evenly coated.

Place the shrimp in the basket of the air fryer, leaving space around each one. Spray on the shrimp on all sides with olive oil.

Air fry in batches at 400°F until crispy, about 6 minutes.

GARLIC-GLAZED SHRIMP

SERVES 4–6

Garlic-Glazed Shrimp is fried shrimp perfected. A simple garlic egg wash gives this classic a flavor boost, and air frying means no oily aftertaste. Serve it with Easy Cocktail Sauce (see page 130), or if you want something a little different, try it with Creamy Lime Dip (see page 136).

2 large eggs

3 garlic cloves, minced

1 teaspoon kosher salt

¼ teaspoon black pepper

1 pound large shrimp, peeled and deveined

1 cup all-purpose flour

2 cups cornmeal

Olive oil cooking spray

In a medium bowl, whisk together the eggs, garlic, salt, and pepper.

Dredge each piece of shrimp in the flour, then dip it in the seasoned egg mixture, and then roll in the cornmeal until evenly coated.

Place the coated shrimp in the basket of the air fryer, leaving space around each one. Spray the shrimp on all sides with olive oil.

Air fry in batches at 440°F until crispy, about 10 minutes.

CRISPY QUINOA SHRIMP

SERVES 4–6

Surprise your taste buds by using quinoa to coat your fried shrimp! This popular grain is healthy and easy to make, and it crisps up perfectly in the air fryer. Throw in a few select spices, and you're on your way to something really delicious.

½ cup all-purpose flour

½ teaspoon ground cumin

½ teaspoon sweet paprika

¾ teaspoon garlic powder

½ teaspoon onion powder

¼ teaspoon kosher salt

⅛ teaspoon freshly ground black pepper

1 pound medium shrimp, peeled and deveined

2 large eggs, beaten

1 cup raw quinoa

Olive oil cooking spray

In a medium bowl, combine the flour, cumin, paprika, garlic powder, onion powder, salt, and pepper.

Dredge each piece of shrimp in the flour mixture, then dip in the egg, and then roll in the quinoa until evenly coated.

Place the shrimp in the basket of the air fryer, leaving space around each one. Spray the shrimp on all sides with olive oil.

Air fry in batches at 440°F until crispy, about 10 minutes.

FIERY SCALLOPS

SERVES 4

Why settle for something ordinary when you can spice things up? In Fiery Scallops, the heat of chili powder and hot sauce plays off the natural sweetness of scallops.

1 cup Homestyle Breadcrumbs (see page 146)

1 teaspoon lemon zest

1 teaspoon chili powder

1 teaspoon paprika

1 teaspoon celery salt

Kosher salt and freshly ground black pepper, to taste

1 large egg

1 tablespoon favorite hot sauce

1 pound sea scallops

Combine the dry ingredients in a bowl, and set aside. In a separate bowl, combine the egg and the hot sauce.

Dredge each scallop in the egg mixture, and then coat thoroughly in the breadcrumb mixture. Air fry at 400°F until golden brown, about 7 minutes.

CITRUSY SNAPPER

SERVES 4

Citrus is well-known for bringing out the flavor in fish, but lime butter takes things to a whole new level. Between the rich topping and flaky fish, this quick dish feels downright indulgent.

1 pound snapper fillets, cut into 4-ounce fillets

1 tablespoon extra virgin olive oil

½ teaspoon kosher salt

¼ teaspoon freshly ground black pepper

½ stick salted butter, melted

2 tablespoons chopped red onion

1 lime, zested and juiced

Lime slices, for garnish (optional)

Brush the snapper fillets with the olive oil and season them with salt and pepper. In 2 batches, air fry at 370°F until the fish is crisp and flakes with a fork, about 10 minutes, flipping halfway through the cooking time.

Combine the butter, onion, and lime zest and juice. Pour the lime-butter sauce over the top of the fish fillets, and garnish with lime slices, if desired.

CLASSIC CRAB CAKES

SERVES 2–4

Old Bay® seasoning was created specifically to complement seafood, so you know it's the perfect addition to any crab cake. Serve Classic Crab Cakes as an appetizer (with a helping of the Classic Tartar Sauce on page 130), or with any of the delicious sides between pages 88 and 114.

1 tablespoon olive oil

1 small onion, finely chopped

1 stalk celery, finely chopped

1 small red pepper, finely chopped

2 tablespoons unsalted butter

1 tablespoon mayonnaise

½ teaspoon Old Bay® seasoning

1 teaspoon fresh lemon juice

1 teaspoon hot sauce (optional)

1 teaspoon Worcestershire sauce

8 ounces lump crab meat

1 large egg, beaten

1 cup crushed butter crackers

Olive oil cooking spray

Heat the olive oil in a saucepan over medium heat. Add the onions, celery, and red pepper and heat, stirring occasionally, until soft, about 3 minutes.

Add in the butter, mayonnaise, and Old Bay®, and cook until the liquid evaporates, about 3–5 more minutes. Transfer the mixture to a bowl, and set aside to cool—about a half an hour on the counter or 10 minutes in the refrigerator.

Once the mixture has cooled, add the lemon juice, hot sauce (if using), Worcestershire sauce, lump crab meat, and egg, and gently fold the ingredients using a wooden spoon, rubber spatula, or your hands.

Place the crushed crackers in a shallow bowl and set aside.

For smaller crab cakes, shape approximately 2 tablespoons of the mixture into a patty. For larger patties, use ¼ cup of the mixture per patty. Press the patty into the cracker crumbs to coat. Repeat until you've used all of the crab mixture.

Place a batch of crab cakes in the air fryer basket, ensuring they are not touching, and spray them with cooking spray. Fry in batches at 400°F until golden brown, about 8 minutes.

FRESH AND FLAKY SALMON FRITTERS

SERVES 3–4

You can't do better than the air fryer for a salmon croquette that's tender inside and crispy outside. Although fresh is best, don't feel guilty if you only have canned salmon. These will be delicious either way (and especially when served with the Classic Tartar Sauce on page 130).

1 (8-ounce) salmon fillet, cut in half

2 tablespoons extra virgin olive oil, divided

¼ teaspoon kosher salt

⅛ teaspoon freshly ground black pepper

2 tablespoons finely chopped fresh dill

3 shallots, finely chopped

1 large egg, beaten

1 tablespoon fresh lemon juice

½ cup Homestyle Breadcrumbs (see page 146)

Olive oil cooking spray

Coat the salmon with 1 tablespoon of the olive oil, place it in the air fryer basket, and sprinkle with the salt, pepper, and dill. Air fry at 370°F for 10 minutes, until cooked through and flaky, flipping halfway through the cooking time.

While the salmon is cooking, heat the remaining 1 tablespoon of oil in a small saucepan over medium heat and add the shallots. Cook until tender, stirring occasionally, approximately 2–3 minutes. Remove from the heat and set aside.

When the salmon is done cooking, let it sit for 3–5 minutes, then mash it with a fork in a bowl. Let it cool, covered, for 15–20 minutes.

In a large bowl, combine the egg, shallots, and salmon. Mix well. Add the lemon juice to the breadcrumbs, and then fold the breadcrumbs into the salmon mixture with your hands.

Scoop about 2 tablespoons of the mixture into your palm and form balls, then flatten them to create patties.

Spray the patties with cooking spray and place them in the air fryer basket, making sure to leave space around each one. Air fry in batches at 400°F until golden, about 8 minutes.

TERIYAKI SALMON FOR TWO

SERVES XX

Skip the restaurant and make this delicious dish at home in no time! Teriyaki sauce is deceptively simple to make, and the air fryer cooks up salmon that's perfectly moist. You can serve the steaks with any side, but Green Beans with Lemon (see page 88) make a great pairing.

¼ cup sesame oil

¼ cup fresh lemon juice

¼ cup soy sauce

2 tablespoons brown sugar

1 teaspoon freshly grated ginger

1 garlic clove, minced

2 (8-ounce) salmon steaks

In a large bowl, whisk together all of the ingredients except the salmon steaks.

Add the salmon steaks and gently toss to coat. Cover the bowl with plastic wrap and refrigerate for at least 2 hours.

Remove the bowl from the refrigerator, and let the fish come to room temperature before cooking. Place the salmon steaks on the rack in the basket, and air fry at 390°F until the fish is crisp and flakes with a fork, about 10 minutes.

SIMPLE FRIED SOLE

SERVES 4

If your family prefers hamburgers, getting them to eat fish likely means frying it. Now you can have light and crispy fried fish without the added oil. Make it a fish 'n' chips night by pairing it with Seasoned Fries (see page 109).

1 pound sole fillets

½ cup all-purpose flour

2 large eggs, beaten

½ cup Homestyle Breadcrumbs (see page 146)

1 teaspoon kosher salt

1 teaspoon freshly ground black pepper

Olive oil cooking spray

Slice the sole fillets lengthwise into 1-inch wide strips.

Dredge each strip in the flour, coating on each side. Dip each strip into the beaten egg, then press each side into the breadcrumbs, coating evenly.

Place the fish strips into the air fryer, leaving space around each one. Season them with salt and pepper, and spray them with cooking spray.

Air fry in batches at 400°F until golden brown, about 15 minutes, flipping halfway through the cooking time.

CHAPTER THREE
TASTY SNACKS AND SIDES

GREEN BEANS WITH LEMON

SERVES 4

Sometimes the simplest dishes taste the best! Just a bit of lemon, salt, and pepper make these green beans sing. For a scrumptious appetizer, serve them with Sriracha Aioli (see page 129).

1 pound green beans, washed and destemmed

1 lemon, sliced in half

Kosher salt and freshly ground pepper, to taste

½ teaspoon oil

Place the green beans in a large bowl, and squeeze the lemon halves (cut-side up to keep the seeds from falling out) evenly over them. Season them with salt and pepper, then drizzle the oil over top, and toss to evenly coat the beans.

Spread the green beans over the air fryer basket. Air fry at 400°F for 10–12 minutes, or until the beans are tender-crisp.

BALSAMIC BRUSSELS SPROUTS

SERVES 2

The air fryer does it again: vegetables that are sumptuously tender inside and crisp outside. Just a few ingredients bring out the best in these Brussels sprouts.

2 cups halved Brussels sprouts

1 tablespoon olive oil

1 tablespoon balsamic vinegar

¼ teaspoon kosher salt

Toss all of the ingredients together in a large bowl until the Brussels sprouts are evenly coated.

Air fry in batches at 400°F for 8–10 minutes, shaking the basket halfway through the cooking time, until the sprouts are browned and crisp.

HONEY-GLAZED CARROTS

SERVES 2–3

This wholesome side dish is sure to please even the pickiest eaters and pairs well with mains like the Marinated Skirt Steak on page 71 and the Fried Pork with Asian Dressing on page 63.

1 tablespoon olive oil

1 tablespoon honey

1 teaspoon soy sauce

3 cups sliced carrots (½-inch pieces)

Kosher salt and freshly ground black pepper, to taste

Combine the wet ingredients in a large bowl. Add the carrots, and toss until they have an even coating of the wet mixture. Season with salt and pepper.

Transfer the carrots to the air fryer basket and cook at 390°F for about 12 minutes, shaking the basket a few times during cooking.

FRIED GREEN TOMATOES

SERVES 4–6

Fried green tomatoes are a Southern classic for a reason—texture and taste combine to make something really special. The reason you use unripe green tomatoes is to keep things crisp and juicy. Older (red) tomatoes don't hold up well when fried.

3 large green tomatoes

2 large eggs

¼ cup buttermilk

¾ cup all-purpose flour

1½ cups Panko Breadcrumbs (see page 147)

Olive oil cooking spray

Kosher salt and freshly ground black pepper, to taste

Cut the tomatoes into ¼-inch-thick slices, and place them onto paper towels to absorb excess liquid.

Whisk together the eggs and buttermilk.

Dredge a tomato slice in the flour on each side, then dip into the egg mixture, and then press each side gently into the breadcrumbs, coating evenly. Spray both sides with olive oil, and season with salt and pepper. Repeat with the remaining tomato slices.

Place tomato slices on a rack in the basket, making sure to leave space around each one. Air fry in batches at 400°F until golden, about 5 minutes.

CHEDDAR-CRUSTED VEGGIES

SERVES 4

In summer, you can find fresh vegetables at almost every turn. Cheddar-Crusted Veggies helps you make the most of them while also making something your family will love. Tip: Try serving these as an appetizer with Creamy Red Pepper Dip (see page 132).

1 medium zucchini

1 medium yellow squash

1 small eggplant, peeled

1 tablespoon salt

2 tablespoons olive oil

½ cup shredded Cheddar cheese

½ cup Italian Breadcrumbs (see page 146)

1 garlic clove, minced

½ teaspoon freshly ground black pepper

¼ cup freshly grated Parmesan cheese

Olive oil cooking spray

2 tablespoons chopped fresh Italian flat-leaf parsley

With a box grater, grate the zucchini, yellow squash, and eggplant. Toss the grated vegetables with the salt, and let them sit in a colander to sweat out moisture for at least 30 minutes and up to 90 minutes. Rinse the veggies with cool water to get rid of excess salt, then pat them dry with paper towels. Toss with the olive oil and Cheddar cheese.

In a small bowl, combine the breadcrumbs, garlic, pepper, and Parmesan cheese, and toss to combine.

Spray the air fryer pan with olive oil, then add the vegetable mixture. Top evenly with the breadcrumb mixture.

Air fry at 350°F until the vegetables are tender, about 25 minutes. Top with parsley.

FRIED GREEN BEANS

SERVES 4

Do you have a picky eater at home? Maybe you're the picky eater? Then you'll want to introduce these crispy, flavorful green beans into your weekly routine. Serve them with a little Sriracha Aioli (see page 129) or Fiery Cucumber Sauce (see page 141) for a creamy flavor boost.

½ pound fresh string (green) beans, trimmed

1 large egg

¼ cup 2% or whole milk

1 cup Italian Breadcrumbs (see page 146)

½ teaspoon chili powder

½ teaspoon garlic powder

½ teaspoon onion powder

½ cup all-purpose flour

Blanch the string beans by heating them in boiling water for 2–3 minutes, then immediately rinsing with cold water to stop the cooking process. Drain the beans, pat them dry with paper towels, and then refrigerate them for 30 minutes.

In a shallow bowl, whisk together the egg and the milk.

In a separate shallow bowl, combine the breadcrumbs, chili powder, garlic powder, and onion powder, and mix well.

Dredge each string bean in the flour, dip into the beaten egg, and then coat evenly with the breadcrumb mixture. Place the beans in the air fryer basket, leaving space around each one.

Air fry in batches at 400°F until golden brown, about 10 minutes.

SUPERFOOD CHIPS

SERVES 4

Superfood kale isn't just a great addition to salads and smoothies—baked in an air fryer with a little olive oil and sea salt, this leafy green transforms into an indulgent-tasting snack. These light and crispy chips will call to you.

1 bunch kale

1½ tablespoons extra virgin olive oil

Sea salt, to taste

Remove the stems from the kale leaves, and cut the leaves into squares of 1–2 inches. Make sure they're completely dry by patting them with paper towels.

Drizzle the olive oil over the kale, and then season it with salt.

Place the kale leaves in the basket of the air fryer, being careful not to let them overlap. Air fry in batches at 360°F until edges are curled and crispy but not burned, about 15 minutes. Let cool before serving.

HOT CASSAVA CHIPS

SERVES 4

When it comes to chips, the crunchier the better—and that's where cassava (or yucca) comes in. Add some spices to this healthy root vegetable, and you have deliciously crispy chips in no time.

2 yucca roots

3/4 teaspoon kosher salt

1 tablespoon chili powder

1 pinch cayenne pepper

Slice the yucca into thin discs using a mandolin, or slice as thinly as possible using a knife. Lay the slices in a single layer on paper towels, and sprinkle the remaining ingredients over them. Let sit for 15 minutes.

Place the slices in the basket of the air fryer, making sure they don't overlap. Air fry in batches at 360°F until crispy, about 25 minutes. Shake the basket to flip the chips 1 or 2 times during the cooking time.

CHEESY ZUCCHINI CHIPS

SERVES 2

Turn your favorite side dish (Zucchini Cakes, page 16) into your favorite snack just by slicing your zucchini extra thin. The Parmesan-breadcrumb coating becomes a crust for a perfectly crispy chip.

2 medium zucchini

1 tablespoon salt

½ cup Italian Breadcrumbs (see page 146)

½ cup freshly grated Parmesan cheese

1 large egg, beaten

Canola oil cooking spray

Kosher salt and freshly ground black pepper, to taste

Slice the zucchini into thin discs using a mandolin slicer, or slice as thinly as possible using a knife. Toss the zucchini slices with the salt, and let drain in a colander for 30 minutes. Rinse thoroughly with cold water to get rid of any excess salt. Then lay the zucchini slices on paper towels, and pat them dry.

In a shallow bowl, combine the breadcrumbs and Parmesan cheese. Dip the zucchini slices in the egg, and then dredge on each side in the breadcrumbs to coat thoroughly. Spray on each side with canola oil.

Place the slices in the basket of the air fryer, making sure they don't overlap. Air fry in batches at 390°F until crispy, about 10 minutes. Season with salt and pepper to taste.

PARMESAN VEGGIE CHIPS

SERVES 2

If you think ordinary potato chips are addicting, just wait until you try these Parmesan Veggie Chips! Serve them up with Marinara Dipping Sauce (see page 131) for all the hearty flavor of an eggplant Parmesan.

1 large eggplant, peeled

2 teaspoons kosher salt

1 large egg, beaten

2 tablespoons whole milk

2 cups Panko Breadcrumbs
(see page 147)

½ cup freshly grated Parmesan
cheese

Olive oil cooking spray

Slice the eggplant lengthwise into quarters, and then slice each section widthwise as thinly as possible to make the chips. Toss the chips with the salt, and let sit in a colander to drain for 30 minutes. Rinse the chips in cool water to remove excess salt, and lay on paper towels to dry. Once dry, place the chips on a cookie sheet and freeze for 1 hour.

In a shallow bowl, whisk together the egg and milk.

In a separate shallow bowl, mix together the breadcrumbs and Parmesan cheese.

Remove the eggplant chips from the freezer. Dip each one into the egg mixture, then dredge each side in the breadcrumb mixture, coating well. Shake off any excess breadcrumbs.

Place the chips in the basket, making sure they don't overlap. Spray all sides with olive oil. Air fry in batches at 400°F until crispy, about 5 minutes.

FRIED PICKLE CHIPS

SERVES 4

The bite of dill pickles meets the crunch of breadcrumbs for a guilt-free snack you'll love. Pair these adorably dippable little chips with Fiery Cucumber Sauce (see page 141) or Perfect Burger Sauce (see page 129).

1 (32-ounce) jar large whole dill pickles

2 large eggs, beaten

⅔ cup Panko Breadcrumbs (see page 147)

⅓ cup grated Parmesan

¼ teaspoon dried dill weed

Cut the pickles on the diagonal into ¼-inch-thick slices. Pat them dry using paper towels.

In a shallow bowl, combine the breadcrumbs, Parmesan, and dill weed. Dip each pickle slice in egg, then dredge it on both sides in the breadcrumb mixture to coat thoroughly.

Air fry the pickles in single-layer batches at 360°F for 8–10 minutes, shaking the basket halfway through the cooking time to flip them.

PLANTAIN CHIPS

SERVES 3–4

Not a fan of bananas? Try Plantain Chips anyway. When prepared in the air fryer with a little bit of olive oil, salt, and pepper, these savory counterparts are more addictive than potato chips (and much healthier).

2 green plantains

1 tablespoon extra virgin olive oil

Kosher salt and freshly ground black pepper, to taste

Peel and slice the plantains into thin discs using a mandolin slicer, or slice as thinly as possible using a knife. Brush each slice with the olive oil on both sides.

Place the plantain slices in the basket of the air fryer, making sure they don't overlap.

Air fry in batches at 360°F until crispy, about 25 minutes. Season with salt and pepper to taste.

SWEET ONION RINGS

SERVES 4

Onion rings don't need much to taste amazing, but using a sweet Vidalia onion instead of other varieties makes these irresistible. While you can use traditional breadcrumbs if you like, Panko Breadcrumbs give the onion rings a crunchier bite.

1 small Vidalia onion, peeled and sliced into 1/8-inch rounds

1 cup self-rising flour

1 teaspoon kosher salt, plus additional for seasoning

1/2 teaspoon freshly ground black pepper

2 large eggs, beaten

1 cup Panko Breadcrumbs (see page 147)

Canola oil cooking spray

Soak the onion slices in ice water for 30 minutes to firm them up and seal in their flavor. Drain in a colander.

In a large bowl, combine the flour, salt, and pepper, and toss gently to combine. Dredge each of the onion rings in the flour mixture, then dip into the beaten egg, and then coat evenly with the breadcrumbs. Shake off any excess coating, and spray each ring with canola oil.

Place the onion rings in the air fryer basket, making sure to leave room around each one. Air fry in batches at 400°F until golden, about 7 minutes. Season with additional salt to taste.

PARMESAN CAULIFLOWER TOTS

SERVES 3

If you're looking for a healthy alternative to potatoes, you can't do any better than cauliflower. With riced cauliflower available just about anywhere, recipes like this one are deliciously simple.

2 cups riced cauliflower

2 large eggs

1/4 cup breadcrumbs

1/4 cup Parmesan cheese

1/4 teaspoon onion powder

1 teaspoon Italian seasoning

Add all of the ingredients to a large bowl, and mix until well combined. Using your hands, form the dough into small nuggets, or tots. Air fry them in one layer at 400°F for 10 minutes.

Sweet Onion Rings

DINER-STYLE HOME FRIES

SERVES 4

Home fries are arguably the best thing about a classic diner menu. With Diner-Style Home Fries, you get all the flavor and none of the grease, and you don't even have to leave home.

3 large potatoes, scrubbed and diced into ½-inch cubes

2 tablespoons olive oil

2 teaspoons kosher salt

1 teaspoon onion powder

1 teaspoon garlic powder

1 teaspoon paprika

1 medium onion, diced

1 small green pepper, diced

Add the diced potatoes to a large bowl, cover with water, and soak them for 20–30 minutes.

Drain the potatoes, dry them, and return them to the now empty and dry bowl. Add the olive oil to the bowl and toss with the potatoes to coat, before transferring them to the air fryer basket. Air fry the potatoes at 370°F for 20 minutes, shaking the basket several times during cooking. Meanwhile, combine the salt, onion powder, garlic powder, and paprika in a small bowl and set it aside.

At the end of the cooking time, return the potatoes to the large bowl. Add in the onions and peppers, then toss them with the seasoning mixture to coat. Transfer the mixture back to the air fryer basket and cook at 380°F for 5–10 more minutes, shaking the basket once or twice, until the potatoes are browned and the vegetables are tender.

SCALLOPED POTATOES

SERVES 4–6

Whoever first combined potatoes with cheese should be given some kind of award. These potatoes au gratin are made with Gruyère cheese for a hint of creamy sweetness that really takes them up a notch.

½ cup whole milk

½ cup cream

½ cup Parmesan cheese

1 garlic clove, diced

½ teaspoon freshly grated nutmeg

½ teaspoon kosher salt

1 teaspoon freshly ground black pepper

3 medium russet potatoes, peeled and thinly sliced (⅛-inch thick or thinner)

Canola oil cooking spray

½ cup grated Gruyère cheese

In a large bowl, whisk together the milk, cream, Parmesan, garlic, nutmeg, salt, and pepper. Add the potato slices, and mix well to coat.

Spray the bottom of the air fryer pan with canola oil. Then pour the potato mixture into the pan.

Air fry at 390°F for 10 minutes, then top with the Gruyère. Continue frying until the cheese is bubbly and begins to brown, about 5 minutes.

ROASTED RED POTATOES

SERVES 4–6

With just a few fresh ingredients and an air fryer, you can create delicious roasted potatoes in no time. Rosemary is a wonderful complement to pork, so try these with the Honey Mustard Pork on page 60.

2 pounds small red potatoes

1 tablespoon extra virgin olive oil

1 teaspoon kosher salt

½ teaspoon freshly ground black pepper

1 teaspoon dried rosemary

1 tablespoon chopped fresh rosemary

Halve or quarter the potatoes to make bite-size pieces.

In a large bowl, toss the potato pieces with the olive oil, salt, pepper, and dried rosemary until thoroughly coated.

Air fry the potatoes in batches, placing them in a single layer in the basket. Start out at 360°F for 10 minutes. Then shake the basket to flip the potatoes, and air fry at 400°F until they are cooked through, about 10–15 minutes more. Top with the fresh rosemary.

GARLICKY BAKED POTATOES

SERVES 2–3

Your air fryer makes perfect baked potatoes, so why not have a little fun with it? Dress them up with a little garlic and parsley, then top them off with sour cream and enjoy!

3 Idaho or russet baking potatoes

1½ tablespoons olive oil

1 tablespoon kosher salt

1 tablespoon garlic

1 teaspoon parsley

Rinse and dry the potatoes, and use a fork to create a few holes in each for the air to escape from.

Combine the rest of the ingredients in a small bowl. Brush each potato with the mixture, and then rub it in to coat evenly using your hands.

Transfer the potatoes to the air fryer, and cook them at 392°F for 35–40 minutes or until they are tender.

Roasted Red Potatoes

GARLIC PARMESAN POTATOES

SERVES 6

These mouthwatering potatoes are the perfect complement to the Marinated Skirt Steak on page 71, but they're so delicious that you may start looking for excuses to make them.

3 pounds red potatoes

1/2 teaspoon basil, dried

5 cloves garlic, minced

1/2 teaspoon oregano, dried

2 tablespoons chopped parsley leaves

1 teaspoon thyme, dried

Kosher salt and freshly ground black pepper, to taste

2 tablespoons olive oil

2 tablespoons unsalted butter, melted

1/3 cup Parmesan cheese, grated

Clean and quarter the potatoes, then transfer them to a large bowl. Add the remaining ingredients to the bowl, and mix well to evenly coat the potatoes.

Air fry the potatoes in single-layer batches at 400°F for 18–20 minutes, shaking the basket to flip the potatoes halfway through the cooking time. The potatoes are done when they are crisp and golden brown.

POTATO PANCAKES

SERVES 4

If you like hash browns, you'll love Potato Pancakes. The difference is just egg and flour, but potato pancakes (or latkes) are both a European and Jewish tradition, and a delightful comfort food you can serve up with any meal.

2 medium or large russet potatoes, peeled

1 small onion

1 large egg, beaten

1 teaspoon kosher salt

½ teaspoon freshly ground pepper

3 tablespoons all-purpose flour

Put the potatoes in a pot, and cover them with water. Bring the water to a boil, and cook the potatoes for about 10 minutes, until you can just sink a fork into them (they should still be firm). Drain and let them cool enough to handle.

Using a box grater, grate the onion and potatoes, and toss them together to combine. Place the grated mixture in a tight mesh strainer, and press the mixture to release excess liquid. Blot the mixture with a paper towel, and transfer it to a large bowl.

Add the egg, salt, and pepper, and stir with a fork to mix. Next, add 1 tablespoon of flour at a time, mixing thoroughly between each addition.

Scoop about ¼ of the mixture into the palm of your hand, and form it into a patty. Repeat with remaining mixture. Place 1 patty at a time in the air fryer basket.

Air fry in batches at 400°F until golden brown, about 20 minutes.

Seasoned Fries

SEASONED FRIES

SERVES 4–6

If you prefer your French fries thick and pillowy, the air fryer is the tool for you! It creates a crisp outer shell and fluffy interior every time. Seasoned Fries adds some interest to basic French fries with just a hint of heat.

4 medium russet potatoes, sliced into ¼-inch thick strips

3 tablespoons extra virgin olive oil

1 teaspoon sweet or smoked paprika

¼ teaspoon kosher salt

¼ teaspoon freshly ground black pepper

½ teaspoon chopped fresh Italian flat-leaf parsley

Soak the potato strips in ice water for 1 hour to remove the starch, then drain them in a colander.

Place the strips in the air fryer basket, making sure to leave space around each one, and air fry in batches at 400°F for 15 minutes. Then remove them from the air fryer, and let them cool at room temperature for 10 minutes.

Toss the strips with the olive oil, paprika, salt, and pepper. Then transfer them back to the basket, and continue to air fry in batches at 400°F until golden brown, about 15 more minutes. Top with the parsley.

YOUR NEW FAVORITE FRIES

SERVES 3–4

Once you learn how to make mouthwatering fries at home, you'll never need to hit the drive-thru again. Want to know the professionals' secret? Frying them twice!

2 medium russet potatoes, peeled and sliced into ¼-inch- thick strips

1 tablespoon peanut or canola oil

1 teaspoon kosher salt

Soak the potato strips in ice water for 1 hour to remove the starch, and then drain them in a colander.

Place the strips in the air fryer basket, making sure to leave space around each one, and air fry in batches at 400°F for 15 minutes. Then remove them from the air fryer, and let them cool at room temperature for 10 minutes.

Toss the strips with the oil and salt. Then transfer the strips back to the basket and continue to air fry in batches at 400°F until golden brown, about 15 more minutes.

SWEET POTATO FRIES

SERVES 3–4

Sweet Potato Fries are a healthy side your whole family will love. Adding a little heat in the way of cumin and cayenne pepper balances out the natural sweetness of the vegetable, and air frying it twice gives you a craveable crunch.

2 large sweet potatoes, peeled and sliced into ¼-inch thick strips

1 tablespoon extra virgin olive oil

1 teaspoon ground cumin

1 pinch cayenne pepper

½ teaspoon kosher salt

Soak the sweet potato strips in ice water for 1 hour to remove the starch, then drain them in a colander.

Place the strips in the air fryer basket, making sure to leave space around each one, and air fry in batches at 400°F for 15 minutes. Then remove them from the air fryer, and let them cool at room temperature for 10 minutes.

Toss the strips with the olive oil, cumin, cayenne pepper, and salt. Then transfer them back to the basket and continue to air fry in batches at 400°F until golden brown, about 15 more minutes.

SPICED SWEET POTATO CHIPS

SERVES 4–5

It's hard to top the naturally delicious taste of sweet potatoes, but Spiced Sweet Potato Chips brings the heat you need to do just that. These chips are great alone, and even better when paired with a cool sauces like Creamy Lime Dip (see page 136).

2 large sweet potatoes, peeled

1 tablespoon olive oil

1 tablespoon smoked paprika

1 tablespoon garlic powder

½ tablespoon light brown sugar

½ tablespoon onion powder

½ teaspoon chili powder

1 teaspoon kosher salt

1 teaspoon freshly ground black pepper

Slice the sweet potatoes into thin discs using a mandolin slicer, or slice as thinly as possible using a knife.

In a large bowl, toss the sweet potato slices with the olive oil to thoroughly coat. Add the remaining ingredients, and toss to coat.

Place the potato slices in the basket of the air fryer, making sure they don't overlap. Air fry in batches at 390°F until crispy, about 12 minutes.

HERB-CRUSTED POTATO CHIPS

SERVES 2–4

This grown-up take on potato chips, with an assortment of savory herbs, may ruin the store-bought variety for you.

2 medium russet potatoes

1 tablespoon extra virgin olive oil

1 teaspoon dried rosemary

1 teaspoon dried thyme

1 teaspoon dried oregano

1 teaspoon kosher salt

Slice the potatoes into thin discs using a mandolin slicer, or slice as thinly as possible using a knife.

Place the potato slices into a bowl of ice water and let soak for 30 minutes. Drain them in a colander, then pat them dry with paper towels.

In a large bowl, toss the potato slices with the olive oil.

Place the potatoes in the basket of the air fryer, making sure they don't overlap. Air fry in batches at 330°F until crispy, about 30 minutes.

While the chips are still warm, toss them with the remaining ingredients, and serve.

CHAPTER FOUR
DELECTABLE
DESSERTS

HONEYED APPLE TARTS

SERVES 15

Impress your guests with these delectable little tarts that taste elegant and whip up in no time. Fresh ingredients and zero oil mean these are virtually guilt-free little treats.

3 small baking apples, such as Gala, Granny Smith, or Golden Delicious

2 teaspoons raw honey

1/8 teaspoon cinnamon

1 teaspoon lemon zest

1 teaspoon fresh lemon juice

1 tablespoon unsalted butter, melted

1 (10- x 15-inch) sheet frozen or refrigerated puff pastry dough, thawed but still cool

1 large egg, beaten

Core and peel the apples, and chop them into 1/4-inch cubes. Set them aside.

In a large bowl, combine the honey, cinnamon, lemon zest, lemon juice, and melted butter, and stir well to combine. Add the apple cubes, and toss to coat well.

Using a pizza cutter, slice the puff pastry sheet into 15 squares of roughly the same size.

Spoon a heaping teaspoon of the apple mixture into the center of each square. Using the tip of your finger or a brush, apply a small amount of the beaten egg to all the edges of each square, like a frame.

Form the tartlets into dumpling shapes by pulling up two opposite corners and pinching them together, then pinching together the other corners.

Place the tartlets in the basket of the air fryer, leaving plenty of room around each one. Air fry in batches at 360°F until golden brown, about 20 minutes.

BAKED APPLES

SERVES 2

The comforting flavors of fall converge in this delicious-but-healthy dessert that's perfect for two. Change things up by using pears instead of apples for an equally scrumptious treat.

1 medium apple

1½ teaspoons light margarine, melted

¼ teaspoons cinnamon

¼ teaspoons nutmeg

2 tablespoons chopped walnuts

2 tablespoons raisins

¼ cup water

Cut the apple in half horizontally, and scoop out the seeds and some of the fruit. Place both halves hole-side up in the baking pan.

Combine the margarine, cinnamon, nutmeg, walnuts, and raisins in a small bowl, then spoon this mixture into apple halves.

Pour the water into the pan, and air fry at 350°F for 20 minutes.

CINNAMON APPLE CHIPS

SERVES 2–4

Looking for a guilt-free snack or dessert to satisfy your sweet tooth? These chips will hit the spot without hurting your waistline. Plus, leaving the peels on ensures you get all the nutrients of the apple.

2 Gala apples

2 tablespoons unsalted butter, melted

1 teaspoon ground cinnamon

2 teaspoons light brown sugar

Core the apples and slice them into thin discs using a mandolin slicer, or slice as thinly as possible using a knife.

Lay the apple slices on a clean work surface and drizzle them with the melted butter, then sprinkle them with the cinnamon and brown sugar.

Place the apple slices in the basket of the air fryer, making sure they don't overlap.

Air fry in batches at 360°F until crispy, about 25 minutes. Shake the basket to flip the chips 1 or 2 times during cooking time.

SEASONAL FRUIT CRISP

SERVES 2–4

Talk about comfort food! The best part about Seasonal Fruit Crisp is the ability to customize your crisp with whatever fruit combination you like best—maybe peaches and almonds, or apples and cinnamon.

1 cup raspberries

1 cup blueberries

1 teaspoon fresh lemon juice

¼ cup granulated sugar, divided

¼ cup all-purpose flour

½ cup rolled oats

¼ teaspoon pure vanilla extract

¼ cup dark brown sugar

3 tablespoons cold unsalted butter, sliced into chunks

Canola oil cooking spray

In a large bowl, combine the raspberries, blueberries, lemon juice, and ½ of the granulated sugar. Toss gently to coat the berries.

In a medium bowl, combine the flour, oats, vanilla extract, brown sugar, and remaining granulated sugar. Then mash the butter into the mixture, piece by piece, until the mixture becomes crumbly.

Spray the air fryer pan with canola oil, and pour the raspberry-blueberry mixture into the pan. Then sprinkle the butter-flour mixture evenly over the top.

Air fry at 390°F until the crumble is golden brown and the fruit is bubbly, about 12 minutes.

RASPBERRY HAND PIES

SERVES 10–12

With fresh raspberries and flaky dough, these little pies beat out the store-bought kind any day of the week. If your sweet tooth is still aching, top them off with the glaze used on the Vanilla-Glazed Doughnuts on page 34.

1 cup chopped raspberries

2 tablespoons granulated sugar

2 teaspoons cornstarch

1 teaspoon lemon juice

¼ teaspoon pure vanilla extract

1 pinch kosher salt

1 (20-ounce) package frozen empanada wrappers, thawed

1 large egg, beaten

Canola oil cooking spray

In a medium bowl, combine the raspberries, sugar, cornstarch, lemon juice, vanilla extract, and salt.

Lay out the empanada wrappers on a floured countertop. Using the tip of your finger or a brush, apply a small amount of the egg to the edges of each wrapper.

Spread a heaping tablespoon of pie filling over each wrapper, then fold each wrapper in half, and press the edges together with the tines of a fork.

Place the pies in the air fryer basket, leaving plenty of space around each one. Spray the pies on all sides with canola oil. Air fry in batches at 360°F until golden brown, about 20 minutes. Let cool for 15–20 minutes before serving.

WHITE CHOCOLATE CHEESECAKE BITES

SERVES 8

What better way is there to enjoy fresh summer fruit than wrapped up in cheesecake and puff pastry? White Chocolate Cheesecake Bites calls for berries, but feel free to sub in whatever fruit calls to you.

4 ounces cream cheese

½ cup granulated sugar

2 large eggs

½ teaspoon vanilla

2 tablespoons chopped white chocolate

½ cup chopped strawberries, blueberries, raspberries, and/or blackberries

1 (10- x 15-inch) sheet refrigerated or frozen puff pastry dough, thawed

Canola oil cooking spray

In a large mixing bowl, combine the cream cheese and sugar. Beat on medium until well blended. Continuing to beat on medium, add 1 of the eggs, then the vanilla. Blend until well mixed, about 1–2 minutes more. Fold in the white chocolate and berries.

Place the puff pastry on a floured work surface with the longer edge closest to you. Using a pizza cutter, cut the pastry in half horizontally, then make 3 equally spaced cuts vertically to form 8 rectangular pieces.

In a small bowl, beat the remaining egg. Using the tip of your finger or a brush, apply a small amount of the egg to all the edges of each rectangle, like a frame.

Spoon a scant tablespoon of the cream cheese mixture onto the bottom half of each rectangle just above the egged edge. Fold the top half of the rectangle over the cream cheese mixture to form a square. Press the tines of a fork along all 4 edges of the square. Repeat with the remaining dough and filling.

Place the dough squares in the basket of the air fryer, leaving plenty of room around each one. Spray them on all sides with canola oil. Air fry at 360°F until golden brown, about 10–15 minutes.

MINI CHURROS

SERVES 4–6

Get the flavor of the fairgrounds without all the unhealthy oil! Mini Churros uses a pastry piping bag and star tip, but if you don't have one handy, you can always just roll the churros out by hand.

1 cup water

½ cup unsalted butter

¼ teaspoon salt

1 cup all-purpose flour

3 large eggs

¼ cup sugar, for coating

¼ cup cinnamon, for coating

Add the water to a medium pot and bring it to a boil. Mix in the butter, salt, and flour, then turn off the heat. Stir in the eggs one at a time until you have a fluffy dough.

Using either a piping bag with a star tip or your hands, create the mini churros (about ½ inch by 1½ inches each) on the air fryer baking sheet. Air fry at 410°F for 6 minutes until golden.

Fill a small bowl with the sugar and the cinnamon, roll the churros in it to coat, and serve them warm.

CHOCOLATEY NUT BUTTER TURNOVERS

SERVES 6

The combination of chocolate and peanut butter is dessert perfection, but it's nothing new. Throw some chocolate-hazelnut spread into the mix, and now you've got something even more interesting—and doubly delicious!

1 (10- x 15-inch) sheet frozen or refrigerated puff pastry dough, thawed but still cool

3 tablespoons creamy peanut butter

3 tablespoons chocolate-hazelnut spread

1 large egg, beaten

On a piece of parchment paper or a clean, floured work surface, lay out the puff pastry dough. Using a pizza cutter, slice the dough into 6 equal squares.

Drawing an imaginary line on the diagonal through each dough square, spread peanut butter on one half and chocolate-hazelnut spread on the other. Fold the pastry on the diagonal line to create a triangle. Press the dough together with the tines of a fork to seal.

Brush both sides of the triangles with the egg, and place them in the air fryer basket, leaving space around each one. Air fry in batches at 360°F until golden brown, about 15 minutes. Let cool before serving.

CHOCOLATE CAKE FOR ONE

SERVES 1–2

When you're craving something sweet but don't have any baked goods handy, you're only a few ingredients away from a plateful of rich chocolate cake. Sure, you could share it with someone else—but you might not want to.

1½ cups all-purpose flour

¾ cup granulated sugar

3 tablespoons unsweetened cocoa powder

1 teaspoon baking soda

½ teaspoon kosher salt

1 teaspoon pure vanilla extract

¼ cup canola oil

1 cup water

1 tablespoon white vinegar

Canola oil cooking spray

Whipped cream, optional

Berries, optional

In a large bowl, combine all of the ingredients except the cooking spray and optional ingredients until just blended using an electric hand mixer.

Spray the air fryer's pan with the cooking spray, and pour the cake mixture into the pan. Air fry at 330°F until a toothpick inserted into the middle of the cake comes out clean, about 30 minutes.

Remove the cake from the air fryer, and let it sit another 30 minutes to cool. Top with whipped cream and berries, if desired.

DOUBLE-CHOCOLATE MACADAMIA NUT BROWNIES

SERVES 4–6

What do you get when you combine a rich, chocolatey brownie with a white-chocolate macadamia-nut cookie? Heaven in a bite. You may want to make two batches of these!

1 large egg

⅓ cup granulated sugar

1 teaspoon pure vanilla extract

⅓ cup semi-sweet chocolate chips

1 tablespoon salted butter

⅓ cup self-rising flour

2 tablespoons white chocolate chips

2 tablespoons chopped macadamia nuts

Canola oil cooking spray

In a large mixing bowl, whisk the egg. While continuing to whisk, add the sugar. When fully incorporated, add the vanilla extract and continue to whisk until well combined. Set aside.

In a small saucepan over medium-low heat, melt the semisweet chocolate chips with the butter, stirring constantly but gently. When fully melted and combined, pour the chocolate mixture over the sugar mixture and fold in to combine thoroughly. Then stir in the flour. Finally, add the white chocolate chips and macadamia nuts, and stir until well combined.

Spray the air fryer pan with canola oil, and pour the mixture into the pan. Air fry at 360°F until the top of the brownies is firm, about 20 minutes. Let cool for at least 30 minutes before slicing the brownies into sections and serving.

CHAPTER FIVE
SAUCES
AND DIPS

KICKIN' KETCHUP

Spice up your sweet tomato ketchup, then try this dip with the Parmesan Cauliflower Tots on page 98.

1 tablespoon unsalted butter

2 medium white onions, finely chopped

1 (14.5-ounce) can chopped tomatoes

½ cup light brown sugar

½ cup white vinegar

1 teaspoon ground allspice

In a large skillet, melt the butter over medium heat. Add the onions and cook, stirring occasionally, until caramelized, about 23 minutes.

Add the tomatoes, brown sugar, vinegar, and allspice. Reduce the heat to medium-low and cook for about 30 minutes, stirring occasionally, until the mixture has reduced by half.

Remove the ketchup from the heat and let it cool. Blend it in a food processor until smooth. Refrigerate it for at least 30 minutes before serving.

TANGY MUSTARD SAUCE

Worcestershire sauce gives mustard a more robust flavor, making it a great dip for the Sweet Onion Rings on page 98.

½ cup mayonnaise

2 tablespoons spicy brown mustard

1 teaspoon fresh lime juice

½ teaspoon Worcestershire sauce

In a small bowl, combine all of the ingredients until well blended. Chill for 30 minutes before serving.

PERFECT BURGER SAUCE

What do you get when you combine three of the best things to ever top to a hamburger? An even better topping. Use the Perfect Burger Sauce to top off your Inside-Out Burgers (see page 67).

1 tablespoon mayonnaise

1 teaspoon spicy brown mustard

1 teaspoon ketchup

In a small bowl, combine all of the ingredients until well blended.

SRIRACHA AIOLI

Sriracha's popularity has soared recently, and for good reason. Sriracha Aioli brings the heat and is perfect for serving with any of the fried veggies in this book.

Yolks of 2 eggs

2 garlic cloves, minced

1 tablespoon chili-garlic (sriracha) sauce

1 tablespoon rice vinegar

¼ teaspoon kosher salt

¼ teaspoon freshly ground black pepper

1 cup canola oil

In a medium bowl, whisk together all of the ingredients except the canola oil.

While continuing to whisk, add the canola oil in a slow, steady stream, mixing until well blended and smooth.

EASY COCKTAIL SAUCE

No seafood recipe would be complete without the kick of cocktail sauce. Use Easy Cocktail Sauce with any of the seafood dishes between pages 72 and 83.

½ cup of ketchup

2 tablespoons horseradish

Dash Worcestershire sauce

1 teaspoon lemon juice

Tabasco sauce, to taste

Mix all ingredients in a small bowl until well combined. Cover with plastic wrap, and refrigerate for at least 30 minutes before serving.

CLASSIC TARTAR SAUCE

Why settle for store-bought sauce? While Classic Tartar Sauce would go great with any fish dish, it's especially nice with the Simple Fried Sole (see page 86).

½ cup mayonnaise

3 tablespoons capers

2 teaspoons minced red onion

2 teaspoons chopped fresh cilantro

2 teaspoons fresh lemon juice

In a small bowl, combine all of the ingredients until well blended. Chill for 30 minutes before serving.

STEAK SAUCE

Now that you know your air fryer can make delicious steak, you'll find yourself reaching for this rich homemade sauce all the time.

2 tablespoons olive oil

6 anchovy fillets, drained

3 garlic cloves, minced

2 tablespoons capers, drained

½ cup orange juice

½ cup prune juice

2 tablespoons Dijon mustard

2 tablespoons tomato paste

Heat the oil in a medium saucepan, then add the anchovies and garlic, and cook over medium-low heat, stirring often, about 4 minutes or until garlic is lightly browned. Smash the anchovies with your spoon as they cook.

Add the capers, and cook 1 minute longer.

Add the remaining ingredients, and reduce heat to low. Cook 10 minutes, stirring occasionally. Remove from heat and let cool completely, about 30 minutes.

Pour the mixture into a food processor, and process until smooth.

MARINARA DIPPING SAUCE

This fresh marinara comes together quickly, and freshly packed tomatoes give it an edge over store-bought sauce. Serve it up with any of the yummy Italian-inspired appetizers on pages 4 to 11.

2 garlic cloves, minced

¼ cup extra virgin olive oil

1 (28-ounce) can diced San Marzano tomatoes

¼ teaspoon kosher salt

10 basil leaves, torn

In a large skillet, cook the garlic in the olive oil over medium-low heat until soft, about 1 minute.

Stir in the tomatoes and salt and bring to a boil. Reduce heat to low and simmer, uncovered, for 15 minutes. Stir in the basil leaves.

CREAMY RED PEPPER DIP

Red pepper goes with everything! This dip does double duty as a spread for recipes like Bunless Mushroom Burgers (see page 68).

1 clove garlic, roughly chopped

1 (17-ounce) jar roasted red peppers, drained and roughly chopped

1 (8-ounce) package cream cheese

¼ cup mayonnaise

2 tablespoons lemon juice

In a food processor, pulse the garlic until it's finely minced. Add the roasted red peppers, cream cheese, mayonnaise, and lemon juice, and process them until the mixture is smooth.

Transfer the dip to a bowl, cover it with plastic wrap, and refrigerate it for at least 30 minutes before serving.

SIMPLE VINAIGRETTE

A side salad tossed in this simple dressing pairs perfectly with recipes like Citrusy Snapper (see page 79) and Marinated Skirt Steak (see page 71).

1 large shallot

½ cup sherry vinegar

2 tablespoons Dijon mustard

½ teaspoon kosher salt

¼ teaspoon freshly ground black pepper

1½ cups extra virgin olive oil

Place all the ingredients except the olive oil in a food processor and process until mixed well.

While continuing to process, pour in the olive oil in a slow, steady stream through the pour spout until all of the oil has been fully incorporated.

SESAME-GINGER DRESSING

Whether you're topping off mixed greens or serving this up with Tempura-Style Veggies (see page 27), you can't do better than this craveable Asian dressing. Refrigerate it for up to 2 weeks.

1/2 cup extra virgin olive oil

1/4 cup balsamic vinegar

2 tablespoons soy sauce

2 garlic cloves, minced

2 tablespoons raw honey

2 tablespoons freshly grated ginger

1 teaspoon toasted sesame oil

Place all the dressing ingredients in a food processor and process until smooth, about 1 minute.

THAI-STYLE PEANUT SAUCE

Add just a few ingredients to peanut butter, and you have a wonderful, savory sauce that pairs perfectly with the Thai-Style Chicken Skewers on page 52.

3/4 cup freshly ground or natural-style peanut butter

3 tablespoons hoisin sauce

3 tablespoons soy sauce

2 1/4 teaspoons sriracha sauce

1 garlic clove, minced

1/4 cup water (or more)

Juice of 1 lime

Add all of the peanut sauce ingredients to a food processor and blend until smooth, adding more water to thin, as desired.

THAI SWEET CHILI SAUCE

Don't buy this spicy-sweet sauce at the store! You can make an even tastier version at home in 5 minutes. Use it to top off the selection of spring rolls on pages 21 and 23.

1 tablespoon dried chili flakes

3 teaspoons minced garlic

¼ cup rice vinegar

¾ cup water

2 teaspoons salt

⅓ cup honey

1 tablespoons cornstarch

2 tablespoons water

In a small saucepan over medium-high heat, bring the chili flakes, garlic, vinegar, ¾ cup water, and salt to a boil, and cook for 1 minute, stirring constantly.

Stir in the honey, cornstarch, and remaining water and cook for 1–2 minutes more.

Remove the sauce from heat, let it cool, and transfer it to a storage container. Refrigerate it for up to 2 weeks.

EASY SWEET AND SOUR SAUCE

Who knew delicious sweet and sour sauce could be so easy to make? Toss these ingredients in a bowl the next time you're making Better Fried Chicken Fingers (see page 47).

¼ cup orange marmalade

2 tablespoons Thai chili sauce

2 teaspoons fresh lemon juice

In a small bowl, combine all of the ingredients until well blended.

Easy Sweet and Sour Sauce

BASIL AND PARSLEY PESTO

If you're a pesto person, you'll love this versatile sauce. Try it out with the Fried Ravioli on page 8.

5 garlic cloves

1 cup walnuts or pine nuts

1½ cups chopped fresh basil

1 cup chopped fresh Italian flat-leaf parsley

¼ cup chopped fresh mint leaves

½ cup extra virgin olive oil

Coarsely chop the garlic in a food processor. Add the nuts and continue to pulse. Then add the basil, parsley, and mint, and process until well mixed.

While continuing to process, pour in the olive oil in a slow, steady stream through the pour spout until all of the oil has been fully incorporated. Use immediately, or cover and refrigerate up to 1 day.

CREAMY LIME DIP

Use this simple but zesty crema to top off Chicken Fajitas (see page 45) or cool down wings like the Honey Sriracha Wings on page 28.

1 cup plain yogurt

2 teaspoons lime zest

2 teaspoons lime juice

Kosher salt and freshly ground black pepper, to taste

In a small bowl, combine the first 3 ingredients until well blended. Season with salt and pepper.

ALMOND PESTO

Swapping out pine nuts for almonds gives this pesto a subtler flavor, so it makes a great spread for sandwiches or a dipping sauce for recipes like the Herbed Ricotta Bites on page 10.

¼ cup toasted almonds

2 garlic cloves

2 cups fresh basil leaves

6 tablespoons extra virgin olive oil

½ teaspoon kosher salt

1 teaspoon freshly grated Parmesan cheese

Place the almonds and garlic cloves in a food processor fitted with a steel blade, and pulse until they are well chopped. Add the basil and pulse until combined. While the machine is running, gradually add the oil and process until smooth. Add the salt and Parmesan cheese and process until combined. Use immediately, or cover and refrigerate up to 2 days.

SPICY MAYO DIP

Curry and garlic powders kick this creamy dip up a notch, making it perfect for Sweet Potato Chips (see page 113) or Sweet Potato Fries (see page 111).

¼ cup mayonnaise

¼ cup plain yogurt

1 teaspoon curry powder

½ teaspoon garlic powder

Kosher salt and freshly ground black pepper, to taste

In a small bowl, combine the first 4 ingredients until well blended. Season with salt and pepper to taste. Chill for 30 minutes before serving.

Almond Pesto

FIERY CUCUMBER SAUCE

This take on creamy Tzatziki sauce pairs crisp cucumber with the bite of jalapeño. Try using it to top off the Lamb Pockets on page 64.

⅔ medium English cucumber, peeled, seeded, and chopped

½ cup plain yogurt

¼ cup chopped fresh Italian flat-leaf parsley

¼ cup chopped fresh cilantro leaves

1 small jalapeño pepper, seeded and membranes removed

1 garlic clove, minced

⅓ teaspoon kosher salt

¼ teaspoon freshly ground black pepper

Place all the ingredients in a food processor, and process until smooth. Refrigerate for 30 minutes before serving.

ROASTED EGGPLANT DIP

The flavors of the Mediterranean come alive in this dip, which is perfect for the Lamb Pockets on page 64 or the Greek-Style Arancini on page 6.

1 large eggplant, pricked with the tines of a fork

2 garlic cloves, minced

¼ cup crumbled Bulgarian feta cheese

1 teaspoon chopped fresh oregano leaves

1 teaspoon chopped fresh mint leaves

¼ cup fresh lemon juice

1 beefsteak tomato or 2 plum tomatoes, cored and finely chopped

¼ cup pitted black olives (such as Kalamata, oil-cured, or Gaeta), chopped

½ teaspoon kosher salt

¼ teaspoon freshly ground black pepper

Preheat the oven to 450°F.

Place the eggplant on a baking sheet in the oven and roast, turning often, until it is very soft when pricked with a fork, about 45 minutes. When it is cool enough to handle, scoop out the flesh, place it in a large mixing bowl, and coarsely mash it. Discard the skin.

Add the remaining ingredients and stir until just blended.

CHAPTER SIX
BUTTERS AND CRUMBS

LEMON BUTTER

You can use this rich butter, enhanced with hints of citrus and white wine, on any chicken or fish dish, but it'd also be a lovely topping for a simple baked potato.

3 tablespoons unsalted butter, divided

1 medium shallot, finely chopped

¼ cup dry white wine

2 tablespoons fresh lemon juice

2 tablespoons heavy cream

1 pinch kosher salt

In a small saucepan, melt 1 tablespoon of the butter over medium-high heat, then add the chopped shallot and cook, stirring until soft, about 2 minutes. Add the wine and lemon juice, and heat 1 additional minute.

Add the cream and salt, and stir to combine. Remove from heat, and stir in the remaining butter. Serve warm.

GARLIC BUTTER

The addition of garlic and rosemary makes this butter a perfect complement for pork dishes.

3 garlic cloves

1 cup (2 sticks) cold unsalted butter, sliced into chunks

2 tablespoons chopped fresh rosemary

1 teaspoon kosher salt

½ teaspoon freshly ground black pepper

Place all the ingredients in a food processor, and process until smooth.

ANCHOVY BUTTER

This complex butter will add savory flavor to any dish but is especially well-suited to salmon.

2 teaspoons capers, rinsed, drained, and patted dry

2 tablespoons anchovies

1 tablespoon extra virgin olive oil

2 garlic cloves

1 cup (2 sticks) cold unsalted butter, sliced into chunks

½ teaspoon kosher salt

¼ teaspoon freshly ground black pepper

In a small saucepan, combine the capers, anchovies, olive oil, and garlic, and cook over medium heat, stirring often, until the mixture begins to brown, about 3 minutes. Remove from heat, and let cool for 5 minutes.

Place the caper mixture, butter, salt, and pepper in a food processor, and process until smooth.

HOMESTYLE BREADCRUMBS

You're all set to try your hand at Fried Mac and Cheese (see page 3), but you forgot to buy breadcrumbs. No worries! You can make your own at home in no time.

Fresh or just-stale bread, any variety, crusts intact

If you're using fresh bread, before proceeding to step 2, cut the bread into slices, and place them on an ungreased cookie sheet. Bake in a 300°F oven for 15 minutes, then let cool.

Cut the bread into 2-inch chunks, and place in a food processor, working in batches if necessary. Process until crumbs are about the size of grains of rice. Alternatively, you can place the bread chunks in a resealable plastic bag, and roll a rolling pin over it until the breadcrumbs reach the desired size.

Store in an airtight container in the refrigerator for up to 1 month.

ITALIAN BREADCRUMBS

Give your Homestyle Breadcrumbs a little extra kick for recipes like Mozzarella Sticks (see page 4) and Fried Green Beans (see page 92).

1 cup Homestyle Breadcrumbs (see above)

½ teaspoon dried parsley

¼ teaspoon dried oregano

¼ teaspoon dried basil

⅛ teaspoon garlic powder

Mix all of the ingredients together until thoroughly combined.

PANKO BREADCRUMBS

Japanese-style panko breadcrumbs are light as air thanks to a lack of bread crusts and are a great way to add extra crunch to any breaded food.

Fresh or just-stale white bread, crusts removed

If you're using fresh bread, before proceeding, cut the bread into slices and place them on an ungreased cookie sheet. Bake in a 300°F oven for 15 minutes, then let cool.

Cut the bread into 2-inch chunks and place in a food processor, working in batches if necessary. Process until crumbs are about the size of grains of rice. Alternatively, you can place the bread chunks in a resealable plastic bag, and roll a rolling pin over it until the breadcrumbs reach the desired size.

Store in an airtight container in the refrigerator for up to 1 month.

GARLIC BREADCRUMBS

If you're a garlic lover, swap these breadcrumbs in for the Italian or Homestyle Breadcrumbs in any recipe.

1 tablespoon extra virgin olive oil, divided

1 large garlic clove, minced

1 teaspoon lemon zest

1 cup Homestyle Breadcrumbs (see page 146)

3/4 tablespoon chopped Italian flat-leaf parsley

1 teaspoon kosher salt

1/2 teaspoon freshly ground black pepper

In a small skillet, heat 1/2 tablespoon of the olive oil over medium heat. Add the garlic and cook, stirring until soft, about 1–2 minutes. Add the lemon zest, and cook until fragrant, about 30 seconds.

Add the breadcrumbs, parsley, salt, pepper, and remaining olive oil. Remove from heat, and stir until well combined.

QUICK REFERENCE COOKING CHART

Use this chart as a general reference for the basic time and temperatures required for different types of food. Depending on the size, shape, or brand you use a given recipe, results will vary. Start with this chart as a guide, and find out what works best for the ingredients available to you.

INGREDIENT	QUANTITY	TEMP (°F)	TIME (MIN)	NOTES
MEAT, POULTRY, & FISH				
Baby back pork ribs	½ slab	360°F	30	Rub with oil and seasoning; stand in basket
Bacon	4 slices, halved	380°F	15	Flip halfway through
Chicken, bone-in	2 pieces	370°F	25	Spray with oil; flip halfway through
Chicken, boneless, breaded	4 pieces	380°F	10	Spray with oil; flip halfway through
Chicken wings	8 wings	400°F	25	Toss with oil and season; shake 2 times
Fish fillet	2–4 ounces	370°F	10	Spray with oil; flip halfway through
Hamburger	2 4-ounce patties	360°F	7–14	Flip halfway through
Hot dogs / Sausages	4–6 links	380°F	10–14	Flip halfway through
Pork chops	2 chops, 4–6 ounces each	350°F	14–18	Rub with oil and seasoning; flip halfway through
Rack of lamb	4–6 ribs	350°F	15–20	Rub with oil and seasoning
Steak	2 steaks, 4–6 ounces each	360°F	8–12	Rub with oil and salt; flip halfway through

INGREDIENT	QUANTITY	TEMP (°F)	TIME (MIN)	NOTES
VEGETABLES				
Cauliflower	1 head	350°F	15	Rub with oil and seasoning; add 1 cup of water in the heating chamber
Eggplant	1–2 cups	350°F	15	Toss in oil and seasoning; shake 2 times
French fries; fresh-cut	1 cup	400°F	14	Toss with oil; shake 2 times
Green beans	2 cups	350°F	12	Shake 2 times
Peppers, small	6 peppers	400°F	12	Shake 2 times
Tomatoes, Roma	3	350°F	10	Halve; toss in oil with salt
Tomatoes, grape or cherry	1 pint	370°F	10–12	Toss in oil; shake 2 times
Squash and Zucchini	1–2 cups	350°F	15	Toss in oil; shake 2 times
Sweet potato fries, fresh-cut	1 cup	400°F	14	Toss in oil; shake 2 times

INGREDIENT	QUANTITY	TEMP (°F)	TIME (MIN)	NOTES
FROZEN FOODS				
Cheese sticks	6–8 pieces	400°F	8	Shake once
Chicken, fried	2 pieces	370°F	20	Flip halfway through
Chicken fingers	4 pieces	400°F	12	Flip halfway through
Chicken nuggets	1–2 cups	400°F	12	Shake 2 times
Chicken wings, pre-cooked	8 wings	400°F	20	Shake 2 times
Fish sticks	8 pieces	400°F	10–12	Shake 2 times
French fries; crinkle cut or thick	1–2 cups	400°F	12	Spray with oil; shake 2 times
French fries; thin	1–2 cups	400°F	12	Spray with oil; shake 2 times
Spring rolls	4 rolls	400°F	8-10	Spray with oil; shake once
Sweet potato fries	1–2 cups	400°F	12–14	Spray with oil; shake 2 times

INDEX

Note: *Page numbers in italics indicate Quick Reference Cooking Chart.*